The Written Word and Other Essays

THE WRITTEN WORD
AND OTHER ESSAYS

Lectures delivered before the Centre College of Kentucky

By HARDIN CRAIG, 1875 - 1968.

KENNIKAT PRESS/PORT WASHINGTON, N. Y.

THE WRITTEN WORD AND OTHER ESSAYS

Copyright 1953 by The University of North Carolina Press
Reissued in 1969 by Kennikat Press by arrangement
Library of Congress Catalog Card No: 78-86008
SBN 8046 0551-3

Manufactured by Taylor Publishing Company   Dallas, Texas

ESSAY AND GENERAL LITERATURE INDEX REPRINT SERIES

To the Memory of
Charles Henry Adams Wager

Preface

THESE lectures have arisen from some of my recent and more or less casual interests and can therefore claim little unity or continuity unless it be such as might have come about through my own thought and my own point of view. There is no great hope in that, perhaps, since, from Centre College days on, I have advocated and practiced breadth of scholarship and variety of interest. This is no doubt old-fashioned, but what can one expect? I think I should have felt imprisoned and unhappy if I had had to devote myself to one small aspect of a great writer, much less to a small section of a small writer. To one who had had glimpses of the greatness of Homer and the ancients, of Chaucer and the Middle Ages, and of Montaigne and Cervantes as well as Shakespeare, English literature itself would have seemed a restricted field. (This sounds unpleasantly critical, but it is meant to be so.) Indeed, it has seemed to me that literature by differences in purpose, knowledge, and fashion illuminates itself with an inner light and reveals in kaleidoscopic changes that it itself is nevertheless a unitary thing, not a narrow and contrived thing whose whole design may be plotted out and explained, a thing of many designs and infinite variety—like life itself. This broad doctrine does not flatter the ego of the critic or expositor, for, if he is honest, he will know and understand how little he and his works amount to. I base this humble statement on something I was told while I was a student at Centre College. I have never looked it up and verified it, for, frankly, it never seemed to need verification. I was told that Newton, possessor of great genius, said, after a lifetime of wide-ranging and yet intensive and fruitful thought, that, in the presence of the

great ocean of the unknown, he felt like a child who had
picked up a few pebbles on the seashore.

The first lecture in the series tries to reassure those who
are confused by the din of new communications that there is
a necessary step or stage in mental development in passing
from the spoken to the written symbol and that the reading
and study of books is probably here to stay. The second lecture traces a single trend or aspect, among thousands, and
tries to give practical illustration of the unity of human life
as it appears in literature. The third and fourth lectures are
intimate bits of Shakespeare interpretation. The fifth lecture
is mainly a matter of self-indulgence. I have loved the poetry
of Robert Burns since childhood and have wished my pupils
to love it. It is as simple as that. Finally, in the sixth lecture
I have recorded an ethical discovery I made in the study of
Milton, a discovery that perhaps in an over-academic way I
regard as of great practical importance.

Charles Henry Adams Wager, to whom I have dedicated
this little volume, came to Centre College as Professor of English at the beginning of my junior year. He was a great
teacher, a beacon of light, a man excellently trained, mar-
velously skillful, and, in his nature and outlook, deeply
spiritual. For many years, after leaving Centre College, he
was head of the department of English of Oberlin College;
and, from many casual contacts with Oberlin graduates, I
judge that his career as a teacher is to be regarded as one of
the very greatest in American higher education.

It has been pleasant after more than fifty years to come
back to Danville with something to do. I have met a good
many people whom I knew in those far-off days, and it has
cheered me up to see how young, sweet-tempered, and hos-
pitable they still are.

HARDIN CRAIG

Columbia, Missouri
May 9, 1952

Contents

The Written Word and Other Essays

I

The Written Word

THE HUMAN BRAIN is an incredibly complex mechanism whose organization and activity are, after centuries of study, but imperfectly understood. We do not know its laws or understand its possibilities. It is conjectured that each human brain has about sixteen billion possibilities of ideation, just as if every human being were provided with an instrument adequate to the activities of a great genius. Strangely enough, the brain under compulsion of necessity is phenomenally active in childhood. Consider the task of infancy in learning to talk. The infant learns within a year or two an entire language with the co-ordination of sounds and meanings. There is no mental task in later life of comparable immensity. And again the achievements of the earliest school years are incredible when considered as to their difficulty. A child will learn in the first grade to read and write and to do simple arithmetical operations. My grandson Greer did this last year. Such an operation demands the learning of an arbitrary set of symbols that appeal to the eye, co-ordinate with the ear and the vocal organs, and apply themselves to a very wide circle of meanings. These things are frequently done with the greatest ease, so that they put to shame adult efforts, let us say, to learn to read, much less speak, a foreign language. A. N. Whitehead stresses these points.

What the child has been doing and what he continues to do is to master the means for the utilization of knowledge. This, however, is an unending task that must be pursued as long as life lasts. Man must, as we say, make a picture of the universe, or rather must continue to work on the details and outlines of a constantly changing and constantly growing concep-

[3]

tion of himself and of his environment, so that the brain does not cease its activity but has to deal more and more deeply with what we call complexity. Our sense organs continue to supply us with heterogeneous impressions that need constantly to be sifted. We by and by realize that our sense organs are not completely reliable and that our interpretations of what comes before us are liable to be wrong, so that we are involved in a never-ending quest for certainty. If that quest is sufficiently methodological and careful, we call it science. Ordinarily the task of understanding is not scientific, but the task of foreseeing usually is. Our welfare seems to rest on our ability to foresee. Now, in nature, there is no scale of observation. There is only an immense body of observed phenomena that come to the brain one by one or in small groups. The brain associates them and interprets them as well as it can. This is its function, its danger, and its opportunity. Order is born of disorder, so that man's welfare depends on his brain. By its means he may achieve orientation, or, as we say, grow in wisdom. He must place himself in time and space and in nature and society. Perhaps our limitations are a blessing, since it is impossible to account for all the phenomena pertaining to human life, although there is certainly a better and worse in the adequacy with which we may comprehend and foresee. The prevailing hypothesis on the widest level is that man is set in a vast and long-continued system of the evolution of life on earth and that man is himself a product of evolution. Most of the greatest authorities believe that man is still evolving and that the center of man's evolution is his brain. Some of them even go so far as to believe that the brain itself enters voluntarily into the work of creation and enables man to become an assistant of God in the carrying out of the great plan of evolving nature.

How does man in this vast field of infinitely varied and speechless phenomena proceed to adjust himself to his environment or adjust his environment ultimately to himself?

The process is called symbolization, which proceeds by means of communication. Symbols are very varied and of many kinds. They may be limited to an individual or may be understood by many individuals. Some one object in the physical universe becomes a symbol and carries a message, over and above its manifestation in sense impression, to the upper brain. Symbols may be vague or concrete. They are generally said to have three aspects; they denote something, connote something, and signify or interpret something. When they appear as mental pictures, they are called images. When they appear in language, they are called words. The creation and use of symbols is often said to be the principal difference between men and other animals. Man is described as a symbol-using animal. This is merely an approach to the subject of language with which as teachers and students of literature we are immediately concerned, but it will give you a necessary reminder that words are by no means the only symbols in common use among men. It may even happen that the manner and tone in which words are uttered are symbols added to symbols. Symbols seem to be necessary to the safety and welfare of man in society, and they play a principal part in the evolution of man.

But we in this instance are limited not only to words as symbols but to words in their written forms. Written symbols are originally and perhaps essentially records, and are therefore associated with organized society to a far greater extent than are spoken symbols or words orally uttered. Let me remind you of what is known of the origin of written language. Written language has played a great part in the development of civilization.

The mind has a tendency to make rules or, as we say, set things in order. The patterns for doing this are fully accepted by lazy or indifferent minds; but, since these patterns do not afford satisfaction unless they are in line with truth, certain discontented minds by means of comparison constantly break up the accepted patterns and strive to make new ones. There is thus a continual effort to make new observations and to reconstruct conceptions of the universe, or some parts of it, in line with experience. The normal procedure is by means of words, which thus become symbols of greater and greater truth. Sometimes these words are mistakenly applied and, being generally accepted, last for varying periods, sometimes for centuries. These false dicta, or fallacies, or mistakes, put thinkers on wrong tracks. The history of our culture presents many wrong and misleading beliefs, so that, in literature at least, we need a history of the prevalence of error as well as of the discovery of truth. But, on the whole, the history of our intellectual progress reveals continual invention by trial and error of new and more and more satisfactory rules or laws.

The literary mind has suffered not only from accepted error, but also much from scientific and philosophic dicta that have narrowed the field and restrained the naturally wide-ranging freedom of the human mind. For example, we have been compelled philosophically for centuries to divide the world and the universe into matter and spirit and even to believe that there was no certain truth but that afforded by mathematics and experimental science. We have also been restricted by the hard and formal conceptions of space and time that came in with the era of modern science, and in our particular field the advancement of our literary learning has been controlled or hedged about by sets of too rigid forms handed down remotely from the Greek world. I refer to such ideas as those of comedy and tragedy, romanticism and classicism, and the so-called techniques of this, that, or the other literary manifestation. We students of literature have, although possessed of far greater learning, actually lost breadth of conception and freedom of endeavor since the Renaissance. Moreover, the temptation to proceed with the further refinement of laws and principles supposed to be finally established has been very great, and resentment against innovators has been very quick and very severe. The brain continues to fit its impressions into established moulds, and in an ordered academic or educational society there seems nothing else to be done. Few artists have the power to learn new symbols or, we might say, make new models or remake old ones. Most attempts at revolution have been made by unenlightened minds, and the consequence is that the attempts themselves seem eccentric. We do not like eccentric minds, and it usually seems better to proceed educationally and critically by means of imperfect rules than to follow fads and vagaries. In the study of literature we need sane, well-informed, and powerful minds. To put this in another way we might say that we need originality, such as that of Shakespeare, Bacon, Cervantes, and Fielding. The study of literature in now in an epicyclic stage.

Since this seems to be a true description of our present state in the world of literature, I should like to break the thread of my discourse long enough to explain to you one chief practical direction in which my thought has been tending. I can put it very simply. I have had some contacts with a movement to bring about a closer union of science and the humanities in our academic culture. The opinion I have encountered is this, that it would be an excellent thing and a curative process if scientists could be induced to perfect their culture by the study of arts and letters. This has seemed to me to be exactly wrong, for I think that our intellectual state can be best improved by having the humanists perfect themselves by the study of science—science in its broadest applications and implications. Science and philosophy have had and will continue to have their way with us, and I think it behooves us to know what they have to say. That they present their message badly, imperfectly, or without interpretation has no bearing on the ultimate outcome.

The intellectual processes of the Middle Ages and of the Renaissance were in no fundamental way different from those of our own age. The thought of the Renaissance differed from that of the Middle Ages in quite the same way in which our thought differs from that of the Renaissance. The learned men of the Renaissance had abundant new patterns, mainly derived from the ancient world, so that their rules and laws were more varied and more adequate than had been those of the Middle Ages, and thus they, as well as we, fitted sensory experience into what seemed to them to be the best available patterns and found satisfaction in the process. The new patterns followed by the men of the Renaissance were, relatively speaking, splendid and all the better because the hard definiteness of the age of science had not yet appeared. The men of the Renaissance had not only Greek philosophy and Greek literature, but also vast and noble symbols of life on earth in many aspects as presented by the Bible, newly translated into the vernacular and rendered widely available by the cheap process of printing.

With Descartes there began the dominance of the conception of mind or soul as completely divided from the so-called material world, which thus became more and more a definite region outside of and different in essence from the soul or mind of man. In the thought of the Renaissance, mind had been supposed to permeate the matter of the body and had been a function of that material substance. Each part of the body could both think and feel and could draw to itself what it needed for its welfare. In Elizabethan psychology the soul, and therefore reason, was left essentially free, and it enjoyed its freedom in a vast and relatively undivided field. As regards this unlimited liberty of the Renaissance mind, it makes little difference that the physiology invoked to account for it was erroneous. I do not say that the undeveloped science of the Renaissance was a blessing to mankind. I merely say that, as compared with later ages, the situation was conducive to relatively untrammeled thought and to originality. The discoverer is one whose brain works in new ways, so that it is possible for him to see and describe new connections and to make new comparisons. There were in the age of Queen Elizabeth at least two rather differently directed minds of this highly original order, the minds of Francis Bacon and William Shakespeare. Different as were their fields of operation, there was no essential difference between them. They were both in a true sense original.

Scientists in the seventeenth, eighteenth, and nineteenth centuries turned to mechanistic ideas and pursuits and painted a picture of what they called a real or material world. They assured us with the utmost authority that it was the only world about which knowledge is possible. Within the limits of their hypotheses their statements were undoubtedly correct, and all the world believed them. They forced all men to go about measuring and marking and made modern men into slaves of the clock. Science neglected human values and often denied spiritual values. About this long reign of science one may say with some pertinency that neither the physical sciences nor the biological sciences are now materialistic, that the determinations of science for the last three centuries have dealt, perhaps necessarily, not with facts, but with figments of the brain, that the universally accepted scientific laws narrowed and restricted the field of mental life and therefore greatly affected both literature and the criticism of literature, and that there is now available, though not yet formulated or widely understood, the doctrine of a new freedom. I do not assert that there is a spiritual realm with its own high importance distinct from a material realm. I do not talk in those terms. I say that there is one vastly complicated area of neural and physiological life and that in the natural, though somewhat ignorant, enjoyment of that vast unity the Renaissance was more fortunate than the men of the seventeenth, eighteenth, nineteenth, and twentieth centuries. Learning had not been departmentalized, and there was no inconsistency in having Francis Bacon, or any other man of his age, take all

knowledge as his province. Indeed, that is precisely what
most of them did. Perhaps Homer and other geniuses of the
older world enjoyed the same freedom, and, if this is so, it will
go further than any other circumstance to account for the vitality of the old classics.

Our concern is on this occasion, however, mainly with
written language as a means of communication, for on the
interchange among men of knowledge, feelings, and opinions
must rest the successes of men now and in ages past. By means
of communication man has achieved co-operation leading to
well-being and through it to those emotional agreements that
bind the world together. Through language men are and have
been able to sharpen and render definite and useful to them
the observations of others, indeed, to use such observations as
if they were their own. The accumulations of the past make
up the principal part of our stock-in-trade. Every day is in
itself only a tenth or a twentieth of a day, for the main substance of every day is derived from the past, which continually
operates as an important, though variable, factor in the present. Communication carries forward and criticizes rules, and
rules are the how, the when, the where, and the why of life.
The special habit or function of the brain is the bestowal of
names, names on which the whole or some considerable part
of society may agree. Names are categories, and the law is
that, if communication is to be successful, things must be
correctly identified and classified. Mediaeval and, in part,
Renaissance science was in a primitive state and went no further than this, since their cosmology, or general scheme of
the universe, was authoritarian and supposed to be unalter-
able. But this, which seems a hampering factor, nevertheless
brought with it great freedom.

The most obvious of references are to ourselves and to our
own mental tools, and for most men this fact of obsession with
self constitutes a terminal point no less effective than the theological prohibitions of the Middle Ages or the ideological

prohibitions of the modern communistic state. It is, however, a well-known fact that, as the ability to communicate grows in the individual and in society, accuracy, directness, and completeness are more and more achieved. Originality continues to sprout. Words by connecting things really but not obviously related generate new ideas, and such connections are very largely the discoveries of science and philosophy. Communication in its various forms controls much of our mental life and of our actions, but a certain ability in generalization beyond the limits of our immediate selves is necessary even if we are to be greatly influenced by any communication. Indeed, it is possible that the striking new methods of communication, such as the radio and television, with their mechanical compulsions to clarity, may bring about changes and possibly improvements in language and literature; but so far their ideal has been the spoken word and the seeing eye, and they lack the universality of appeal of written language. Written language speaks to eye as well as ear and by suggestion to all the senses and does so under conditions that provide time for reflection. No invention perhaps has had so profound an influence on historical man as the invention of writing, and the printed book seems still deeply entrenched in the process of human culture. No appeal to the eye alone and no reproduction of oral discourse can as yet take the place of the written word. Written language has a universality, a convenience, an economy, and the possibility of leisurely repetition that all of its rivals so far lack. The main agent in reading is the eye, the coolest and most intelligent of the senses, and in the process of reading there is a constant infusion, not only of visual elements, but of aural and physiological elements as well, that gives reading an organization like life itself, especially since reading affords leisure for the intermixture of experience and acquired learning. The reading habit still takes hold even in the midst of current distractions. Great books, according to Lord Grey in the *Fallodon Papers,* help us live better, attune us to the nature of which we are a part, and make us know ourselves as parts of the scheme of things, "as children of God and brothers and sisters of men." They make us willing to be friends with ourselves.

Perhaps there is no better description of the place of books in civilization than that of Richard of Bury, who lived from 1287 to 1345 and wrote a book called *Philobiblon,* from which I quote:

"In books I find the dead as if they were alive; in books I foresee things to come; in books warlike affairs are set forth; from books come forth the laws of peace. . . . Books delight us when prosperity smiles upon us; they comfort us inseparably when stormy fortune frowns on us. . . . What pleasantness of teaching there is in books, how easy, how secret! How safely we lay bare the poverty of human ignorance to books without feeling any shame. They are masters who instruct us without rod or ferule, without angry words, without clothes or money. If you come to them they are not asleep; if you ask or inquire of them they do not withdraw themselves; they do not chide if you make mistakes; they do not laugh at you if you are ignorant. O books, who alone are liberal and free, who give to all who ask of you and enfranchise all who serve you faithfully!"

That the invention of writing is a regular feature in the evolution of civilization is borne out by the fact that the process always follows the same course and passes through the same stages. There is first the hieroglyph or pictogram. Pictograms are regularly for the sake of ease reduced to ideograms, and ideograms tend to give way to alphabets. Hieroglyphics, mixed, however, with ideograms, lasted in Egypt for three thousand years. The Sumerians and the later Babylonians used ideograms, with some alphabetical features, for thousands of years, and the Chinese have continued to use ideograms to this day, so that the process of change is no regular thing. Indeed, the adoption of an alphabet was something of an invention. At the end of the Bronze Age and the beginning of the Iron Age priests and merchants of Ungerit are said to have agreed upon the use of twenty-nine Babylonian characters as phonetic symbols by which any word at all could be represented or, as we say, spelled. At any rate about the year 1200 B.C. occurred the invention of *the* alphabet at Biblos, a Phoenician city in the Nile delta—twenty-two signs which are basal to Greek, Hebrew, Latin, Aramaic, South Arabian, Sanskrit, and all modern European and many Asiatic alphabets. The occasion for the invention of written language was always the same. The symbols came into use in order to serve the necessities of trade and practical affairs—for accounts, contracts, deeds, and wills. From the earliest times there were a few hero stories, prayers, sacred writings, proverbs, and codes of law; but, for the most part, what we call literature was passed down for centuries by oral transmission. But this easy form of communication, this use of the written word, was not only a convenience, it was also a great initiatory movement in the realization of native talent and the growth of democracy. Up until the time of the invention of the alphabet writing had been a mystery, a trade practiced by specialists. It was now open to all the world. It rendered possible the development of the science, philosophy, and literature of ancient Greece and of the religion of the Hebrews. Let me pause long enough to remark that education still does these things. It is still true that civilized men cannot live without books.

This first lecture of the series is of course difficult, since it attempts to deal with the deepest fundamentals of literature, and I must go still further in order to complete the conception I have in mind. I personally believe, and I should like to make the suggestion to you, that the newest science of our age will eventually produce effects in the fields of literature and literary criticism comparable to those produced by the age of science that extended from Descartes to Darwin. For two or three centuries most producers of literature and practically all literary critics have adhered to wrong philosophies, and their greatness, when they have achieved greatness, has been in spite of and not because of the system of ideas according to which they were invited or obliged to operate. Some at least of the rules and laws of the age of science have been impediments to literature and misleaders of literary criticism. Very often literary men and literary historians and critics have laid down their lines in conformity with man-made systems most of which since the Renaissance have been too narrow to include the whole of life. I believe that the thinkers about literature of the future must cease to categorize in terms of literary forms, in terms of such words as mind, soul, spirit, matter, force, measurement, and literary techniques, but will or must, as Shakespeare did, proceed with an unimpeded observation of life. They will cease to operate under moral and aesthetic concepts. Shakespeare wrote *Othello,* not as a warning against jealousy, but as an account of the behavior and fate of a jealous man, and he wrote *Hamlet* and *King Lear,* not for doctrinaire purposes, but for their significance as stories of human life. He showed no disposition to make his observations into universal patterns.

I should like to bring before you before I close certain ideas that are free from the facile generalizations of the age of science or reason. There seems to be a sort of mixing chamber in the center of the brain whose function is to make connections and to achieve concepts of the whole, in other words, to arrive at a view of the universal. Our bodily organization, including the brain and the nerves, is enormously complicated just as a system, and the facts of its origin render it still more complicated. We acquire our bodily organization, not from two parents only, but from our ancestors, and this organization so acquired is moulded and shaped by our contemporaries and from the earthly experience of mankind. The form, if not the design, of living things is moreover undergoing gradual change. We know from Darwin and his followers that the focus of change is the difference between individuals of the same species. Even all scientists are not equally able to observe, so that the definitions of science must include the definitions of the varieties of men who make them. Progress and development depend on finding and utilizing new environments, or, as we say, on the formation of new associations in the brain. There is no doubt a relation between the development of the individual and the species and this constant introduction of change. Each individual is part of a large, slowly changing organization, and each individual is possessed of a brain, an instrument of universal scope and with the ability to form and retain multitudinous patterns. In such a complicated system one thing particularly stands out: the demand is for universality, and universality and restrictive rules do not go together. We do not need training in techniques and so-called principles, which are, for the most part, merely imperfect generalizations. The conditions called for are freedom of exploration and care and truth of observation. When ages have enjoyed these conditions, they have produced their quotas of great literary minds. When they have been hampered by man-made systems, whether religious or scientific, they have not done so. The scope demanded is nothing less than the whole, the universal, or such parts of it as are in any way available or comprehensible.

What I have said is slightly technical, and possibly crabbed, but it can be said in simpler and more familiar terms. Modern man has insisted on specializing, which, so far as it consists in gaining necessary skills, is entirely justifiable; but it does not demand that a man so specializing should exclude from his mind all the rest of human life and the universe. The brain is versatile enough to take care of the whole and in so doing to improve the special skill. Another way of saying this is that man has always failed to comprehend the greatness of God and has found it irksome and repugnant even to attempt to do so. Man has always insisted on conferring on God his own human limitations. I am only insisting that we should amplify our conceptions of the greatness of God and his works. I can even say this within the lines of the Shorter Catechism:

"Q. What are the decrees of God?"

"A. The decrees of God are his eternal purpose, according to the counsel of his will, whereby, for his own glory, he hath foreordained whatsoever comes to pass."

What I have said in this lecture may seem to you far away from literature and from the understanding of literature, but it is not. I have laid the bases of literary utterance in the fundamentals of communication, an activity on which progress and, to a large degree, happiness depend. I have stressed freedom and universality as the conditions out of which the greatest literary works arise. Beneath what I have said is the idea that the advancement of science in our own century is in the direction of untrammeled freedom of observation and thought in a field of greater and greater universality. The physical and the biological sciences have been forced by their own integrity to abandon the inimical principle of materialism and have reunited the physical and the spiritual in a new and vaster whole. The symbolic logicians promise us a new and more liberal epistemology. Einstein's great discoveries in the region of relativity are sure to affect the life of our minds in many as yet unknown ways. We may expect a period of acceleration with many great changes within a few generations; and, as society and the individuals who compose it change, so also will literature, the written record of man's thoughts and feelings, undergo changes with the times. Meantime, our own points of view may be profitably altered on such subjects as the nature and operation of originality. The fact remains that the producers of literature and the critics of literature breathe the same air we breathe. Whether they realize it or not, they will be denizens of a world in which relativity holds sway, one world, an immaterial world, and a world in which there is an actual truth other than that of mathematics and experimental science. Our study in the future will therefore be of actual men and women in an actual world, and not a study regulated by the figments and limitations of literary critics and professors of aesthetics. Conclusions, except in particular instances, will be less sweeping, but they will have a greater and greater chance to be true. Is it any wonder then that I should advise humanists to study science rather than advise scientists to study the humanities?

To regard any single, even quite plausible and valuable, hypothesis as a completely adequate solution of any important problem in the interpretation of Chaucer or Shakespeare is to narrow the field and to operate as a traditional scientist; to reject all new ideas is to become the victim of anachronistic ignorance. Imagery does not furnish an answer to all questions, and a complete explanation of life records still leaves many things unsolved. After all, it is perhaps safer to think that it was Hamlet who hesitated to kill the King while the King was at prayer and not Shakespeare himself who was guilty of hesitation. Art and artifice do not account for Shakespeare or Chaucer or even Ben Jonson. That Shakespeare was an actor and a man of the theater confers no exclusive rights in the field of interpretation on actors and stage managers. All of these aspects and many more are factors in the process of understanding and revivifying the literature of past ages. Only breadth of knowledge and sympathy coupled with activity of imagination, all acquired by patient effort and true observation, will enable us to know Shakespeare and Bacon; and we may believe that, as we acquire these skills, we shall become more like these great and original geniuses.

II

The Vitality of an Old Classic:
Lucian and Lucianism

How GREAT ARE the world's losses of great literature, through accident, ignorance, or the failure of a mechanical means of communication from age to age, we do not know. But we know that our losses have been heavy. We have nevertheless a salvage of written matters of inestimable value. We know too that this transmission from age to age has not been exclusively mechanical, and that the organization of society has constantly provided a thing that we call influence. This brings us into a vastly complicated field over which there still hangs a dark cloud of obscurity. Much of our traditional wisdom and many of our literary habits may go back to works that were lost two thousand years ago. It is certain that it is the progeny of great literature, quite as much as literature itself, that lives on in our literary habits, discoveries, and impulses. It is the presence and the importance of this strange continuity in the life of great literature that I wish to talk about in this lecture.

I wish to discuss with you what constitutes the principle of vitality in literature. In the first place, is it due to the activity and sponsorship of teachers, critics, and historians of literature? Sometimes, in the individual case, it certainly is; but down below, I believe, is something stronger, something that wells up of itself from age to age. Teachers of literature, critics, and historians of literature, even reverend ministers of the gospel, are to some extent like the iron man on the top of the old-fashioned peanut-roaster. The dress of this figure was painted on in blue, red, and yellow, and he had on his head a handsome cap. He was geared to the revolving cylin-

der of the machine, and he went through all of the muscular
contortions of a man who was winding up a windlass. But
he was not turning that cylinder; he only seemed to be turning it; it was powered by steam, by something you could not
see. What is that something below which keeps old books
and old authors alive? That, it seems to me, is our question.

I do not wish to run this figure into the ground, but I
cannot resist the temptation of asking you if the ultimate
power behind the vitality of the old classics is not the peanuts.
I think in some measure it is, although there is probably no
one single explanation of our continual satisfaction with the
literary works of the past. Even the most popular, most modern, most exclusive of our own works turn out in the end to
be mainly repetitious.

Is this motive force the hidden needs of human life; is it
the *élan vital*, the urge of human nature, that brings this
phenomenon about? Again we say, "Of course it is." We
have to include this elemental curiosity, this search for the
good and for happiness, and to take it for granted; as also on
the part of humanity a constant search for actual advantage.

So we return to our inquiry and ask more specifically, "Is
it a mysterious factor or agent called art?" We must reply
that it cannot be art in any narrow or exclusive sense. The
actual literary art of the original is often obscured by translation, vulgarized by imitation, and unappreciated by readers.
Old classics are often like inventions or tools, tools for thinking or inventions for understanding. The proper study of
mankind is man, and one suspects that much of the vitality of
the old classics is due to the fact that they enable us to search
out and understand human nature, that is, our own natures.
We often say that they have a point of view, which seems to
indicate that they are tools of the intellect, means by which
we may understand ourselves, our fellow men, and the lives
we live. Old classics are somewhat like fables, or, indeed, like
that vast group of words which are derived from the names

and natures of animals, such as the lion, the fox, the ass, the ox, and the cat. All apparently furnished to primitive men tools by means of which they understood themselves. Lions, foxes, wolves, and the like may be said to have points of view, and we have recorded our use of those points of view in the use of their names and of adjectives derived from their names or habits. This fact must record the way in which neolithic man taught himself to think about himself, his neighbors, and his affairs. The same principle seems to appear in memorable stories, such as that of Dr. Faustus, the man who sold his soul to the devil; of Romeo and Juliet, which records how the self-ishness and stupidity of age destroy the beauty, sweetness, and naturalness of youth in the inevitable relation of courtship and marriage; or of King Lear, which reverses the figures in the action and shows how youth in its quest for wealth and power mistreats old age. One thinks of the stories of Job, of Oedipus, of Gargantua and the good Pantagruel, of Don Quixote, of Dr. Primrose; and of Wilkins Micawber. Yes; no doubt old literature lives on, like everything else, because it records the vital or significant experiences of human beings.

There is one more point that is worth making. Is the vi-tality of the old classics due to their appeal to the imagina-tion? Is it the fact that they awaken men, take them out of themselves, that wins for them the approval of generation after generation in a world of incessant monotony? I think this element is certainly present, and, on this occasion, I am willing to leave the matter in the terms of George Santayana, who says, "Whenever the thread of pleasure enters into the web of things our minds are always weaving, a sense of beauty results."

In any case, you and I, who are experienced, are bound to see that the vitality of the old classics is a thing that takes care of itself, and we may therefore cease to worry about it. The classics do live on from age to age, and, although we may in some measure increase their use and although their use is a desirable thing, their life is by and large independent of us and of all we do or can do. Nevertheless, because the subject is interesting, and for almost no other reason, I wish to pursue it further and to introduce a somewhat elaborate illustration of what I have said.

The second century of the Christian era was, taken as a whole, a period of international peace. Hadrian, the Antonines, and, after the brief reign of Commodus, Septimius Severus were the Roman emperors. The age had many faults. Corruption, both social and intellectual, was widespread, but the ills were those of peace and not of war. The Roman empire lay spread round the shores of the Mediterranean, joined together by that sea, so that communication was easy, and men were intellectually alert and enterprising.

Particularly, it was an age when the world went in for higher education and the academic life. There were universities in Asia Minor, at Antioch and elsewhere in the Levant, at Alexandria, on the north coast of Africa, and in Gaul—at Marseilles, Toulouse, and Lyons. The Gaul was open-minded and curious like the Greek, and Greek culture throve in Gaul. The most important seat of learning of all was, of course, Athens. St. Paul's experience there has made this familiar to us. There were also advanced schools in Italy; but probably the Romans, being practical men and destined to make the practical man's hash of the world, cared less for studies than did the other peoples of the empire.

Universities in those days were different enough from modern universities. There were no registrars, no curricula, no degrees and no diplomas, and no fixed course of study. Teachers and students came together and conducted their affairs largely in man-to-man fashion. Famous teachers received high fees and had many pupils; young and obscure teachers had, we may be sure, fewer students and modest emoluments. It is also probable that some ambitious but poverty-stricken students, unable to engage the services of any master at all, picked up such crumbs of learning as they could by attending public lectures and conversing with their more fortunate fellows. There were school buildings, for we know that St. Paul disputed daily in the school of one Tyrannus at Ephesus. But in that kindly climate much of the teaching must have been in the open air. One likes to think of scenes in the market-places of cities beside the blue Mediterranean where masters with their groups of pupils about them taught in the porches of temples, the entrances of public baths, or, after the fashion of the Peripatetics, in academic groves. The studies were mainly philosophy, in its various more or less degenerate forms, and rhetoric; the latter, a mighty subject including, if we may judge from Quintilian, oratory, law, literature, politics, and public affairs. Students and masters, as at the present time, moved freely from one university to another, and then also the world seems to have had faith in higher education. The man I wish to talk to you about is Lucianus Samosatensis.

Lucian was born into this Greco-Roman world about the year A.D. 125 in the Syrian town of Samosata on the Euphrates, situated just where a main highway crossed the river from Antioch to the East. The family to which he belonged was of small consequence except for the fact that his mother's brothers were sculptors, that is, hermae makers. In that wonderful fashion that the Greeks retained, these uncles of Lucian's were at once artists and artisans; for art was still used in making objects of daily and practical use. Museums are still full of hermae pillars, smaller at the base than at the top, formerly set up in market-places of towns, as cornerstones and markers of land, and as milestones on highways. They are normally surmounted by a head of Hermes, the god of traffic, and are objects at once of beauty and use. Lucian tells us that, as a result of family conference, it was decided that he should be apprenticed to his uncle in order that he might learn the trade of hermae maker. He recounts also that at the commencement of his engagement he was given a mallet and chisel, and a block of marble was put before him with the injunction that he was not to strike too hard for fear of breaking the marble block. He struck too hard, spoiled the marble block, and was beaten by his uncle for his carelessness. He went home and told his griefs to his mother, who comforted him. About this time also he had his famous dream in which there appeared before him the contending figures of sculpture and rhetoric, both females, the former in grimy working clothes, with heavy muscular hands (whose weight he had so recently felt), sternly claiming him for a life of toil; the latter with the beauty, grace, and persuasiveness of ancient rhetoric, sweetly inviting him to follow her. These visions (or desires) he made known to his mother, and she decided that he should study rhetoric. This, being interpreted, means that a certain youth, having been put to business, sickened of it quickly and expressed a desire to go to college instead; and that a certain mother felt, then as often since, that her son's wishes merely corroborated her own opinion that her son was a youth of genius. That time the mother was right.

Where Lucian studied is not definitely known—probably at Antioch and Athens, possibly also in Italy and Gaul. He became an accomplished and successful rhetorician, taught, pleaded in the law courts, and had satisfied everybody but himself by the time he reached the age of forty that he had done right in following the beautiful goddess; but Lucian himself was by no means satisfied. The rhetorical aspect of life left him empty. His feeling may be told by his essay on the young rhetorician who came to him for treatment, since he was ill, as Lucian says, from having swallowed a dictionary. Lucian recommends an emetic and advises the youth to read Plato and other serious authors in order that he might fortify himself with ideas instead of merely words. In his perplexity at the emptiness of life Lucian went to the philosophers, but learned nothing; for philosophy was in a bad way. He could find only degenerate, parrot-like representatives of ancient schools—Pythagoreans, who found their salvation in refraining from eating beans; Eleatics, given over to futile debates; Socratics and Platonists, become mere sophists; followers of Aristotle, lost in hopeless detail and mere hair-splitting; and, finally, a lot of woefully degenerate Epicureans. Lucian seems to have preferred before the rest the proud and somewhat offensive Stoics and to have had some respect for their predecessors, the rough and scurrile Cynics; but Lucian declares that he learned nothing from the philosophers. Religion, then deeply corrupted with the vagaries and abominations of Egypt and the Orient, also had nothing to offer; and Lucian declares that, having arrived at the age of forty in his search for truth, he yet knows nothing and is ready to sweep the boards and begin afresh. Our confused modern world enables us to understand his position, and yet he is perhaps not too much to be pitied, after all, in the achievement of so great an idea at so young an age; especially since he had learned much about human life and had acquired a technical equipment of great effectiveness. In point of fact, he was ready, intellectually and spiritually, to adopt the vocation of critic and satirist.

If one wishes to undertake a piece of work in ordinary life, one usually needs a tool, and Lucian proceeded to choose one. His choice was the dialogue, and there must have been just the required degree of shock to public taste in his choice of it, for the dialogue had been given over to serious matters since the time of Plato. Those who were confronted by dialogues must have fled away in haste if they desired pleasure instead of edification. Lucian with his dialogues was like one who wears a shroud to a fancy-dress ball.

For the work in hand Lucian also needed a point of view, just as in any piece of work one must apply tools in a certain way and in a certain direction. Lucian's point of view was a level and unflinching application of common sense to every issue that he treated. It is one and the same throughout, but for purposes of clearness it may be considered under three heads.

In the first place he practiced the logical form of *reductio ad absurdum*. He followed through the consequences relentlessly until the proposition under consideration revealed its falsity. He loved exaggeration in the cause of truth and became, for example, the exponent of the method of making the falsity of a lie apparent by telling a still bigger one. His most popular work belongs to this class. It is *The True Story*, or *Vera Historia*, so called, as he tells us, because there is not a word of truth in it. It is a tale of adventure by sea, land, and sky, a texture of impossible lies, plausible in detail, but actually incredible. He tells how he set forth with a well-manned boat and a skillful sailing-master westward from the Pillars of Hercules; how he sailed merrily on for leagues until a great storm arose, which not only drove him over the sea, but swept him into the sky. There with sails spread he continued to "navigate" until he effected a landing on the Moon. He met the ruler of those regions, one Endymion, and participated with him and his fellow Moonites in a disastrous war against the Sunites—somewhat like the Peloponnesian War. Many other adventures befell him. His ship, for example, was swallowed by a whale one hundred and fifty miles long, with a completely equipped island inside, twenty-seven miles in circumference, with springs of fresh water, fields, vineyards, and temples—a country inhabited by sundry barbarians, such as the Codheads, Mergoats, and Solefeet, who had to be beaten into submission by Lucian and his party. Lucian dwelt there until he grew bored with the place, when he achieved his freedom by the happy device of setting the forest on fire and thus causing himself to be disgorged.

The lying historians and marvel-mongers whom Lucian ridicules are hardly known, but his idea has been so fascinating that the world has never let it die. *The True Story* is the prototype of the imaginary voyage and still stands comparison with the best of its progeny, such as Rabelais' Journey of Pantagruel, the *Voyage à la Lune* of Cyrano de Bergerac, Voltaire's *Micromegas, The Narrative of the Marvelous Travels of Baron Munchausen*, and, greatest of all, Swift's *Gulliver's Travels*. All Danes will know Nils Klimm's *Subterranean Voyage*, and any holiday bookshelf may offer us its Lucianic story, although the book may seem to be only an imitation of Jules Verne, Edgar Allan Poe, or H. G. Wells.

In the second place, Lucian's point of view may be described as the intrusion of the ordinary. No man is a hero to his own valet, and Lucian insists upon looking too intimately into the stories of gods and heroes. It detracts from the dignity of Jupiter, the Father of Gods and Men, to behold him wrangling with his Olympian household, beset by anything but godlike passions, and henpecked by the jealous and sharp-tongued Hera. In his *Dialogues of the Gods* Lucian delights in picturing Zeus as a rather fussy, rather good-natured old gentleman, without any real power or importance. When, for example, Zeus in one dialogue offers to grant a favor to Cyniscus, he lets himself in for a theological discussion and has to admit that gods as well as men are subject to fate. "Why," Cyniscus says to Zeus, "do you forbear to strike with your famous thunderbolt those who rob your temple, as well as pirates, insolent criminals, bandits, murderers, and perjurers; and why do you blaze away at some poor oak, or rock, or unoffending ship's mast, or even at some just and kindly traveler?" Zeus, having exhausted the ordinary conventional arguments, resorts to abuse and leaves in a rage. Cyniscus calls after him and says that he supposes that it is not the will of Fate that he should have his questions answered, even going so far as to reflect on the hard fate of the Fates who have to distribute destiny in a world like this.

The little dialogue between Hermes and his mother Maia shows in very charming fashion how commonplace the life of the Olympians must be. Hermes enters crying like any human child and complains to his mother about how much he has to do. He must arise at daybreak, sweep out the banquet hall, rearrange the couches, and then report for duty to Zeus, passing him the nectar and ambrosia and running errands for him in every direction all day long. He cannot sleep at night as other gods do, but must marshal all the dead men of the day to the realm of Pluto. He has to attend the wrestling school, act as herald on all occasions, and train orators. One of his most constant duties is in looking after Zeus's numerous sweethearts. He is quite done up and tells his mother he would like to be sold as a slave. Maia replies in homely maternal fashion by saying, "You must obey your Father; remember you are very young. I advise you to march off to Argos and Boeotia and not to waste your time; for if you don't you may get a whipping."

Finally, Lucian was fond of a sharpened retrospect. He was a teleologist looking at worldly matters from the point of view of the end. Particularly in his great *Dialogues of the Dead,* he looked at life from the point of view of death; and, although he had many predecessors in depicting the realm of Hades, the abode of the dead, and some of them gruesome enough, never before had Hades been the theater of such realism. How did Socrates conduct himself when he first arrived in Pluto's kingdom? What has the dead Mausolus to say of his tomb in Halicarnassus? Are there not other things for Diogenes to say to Alexander now that they are together again and have so much spare time? How will Alexander and Hannibal agree as to their comparative prowess as soldiers? In Hades dwell the great ones of the earth, long or lately dead, spending their time in ordinary conversation. They are kept well informed on mundane matters; they would not be better served by the Associated Press; their comments are steeped in finality. Death as a leveler and an annihilator is in a position to comment on human endeavor and to indicate human futility.

This suggests Lucian's device, which the world has never forgotten. Many volumes of dialogues of the dead have been written, some of which we know; the idea is still popular. Every presidential campaign produces a number; any magazine may contain one. Landor's *Imaginary Conversations* achieve greatness, beauty, and originality. Some of us recall the well-deserved vogue of *The Houseboat on the Styx*. Hitler, Mussolini, and Franklin Roosevelt have joined Washington, Bismarck, and Napoleon in Hades. We may imagine their minds still at work in the world, as perhaps they are, and thus amuse ourselves by recording their talk with one another.

Lucian does not let us forget that all the dead of every rank, class, age, and sex present the same fleshless, grinning aspect. Aeacus takes the newly arrived philosopher Menippus on a personally conducted tour through Hades and points out the greatest celebrities of antiquity. Menippus wishes to see Socrates, and Aeacus says, "Do you see the man with the bald head?" "All of them are bald-headed," is the reply. "I mean the snub-nosed one," says Aeacus. "The whole lot of them are snub-nosed," says Menippus. The same philosopher, anxious to see the most beautiful woman of the ancient world, says to Hermes, "Point me out Helen of Troy." "That skull is Helen's skull," says Hermes.

> Was this the face that launched a thousand ships
> And burnt the topless towers of Ilium?

Here they come down the easy slope of Avernus. Perhaps there has been a battle on earth today, and the company is large: the old and unwept, those who have never lived, those slain in battle, those killed by accident, those murdered, those who were pestilence-stricken. Hermes is late with his convoy, because Megapenthes has run away and has had to be chased and recaptured. Megapenthes is in chains, still pleading to be allowed more time on earth; for he wishes to finish his walls and his docks and to give his wife instructions about his buried treasure. He offers to bribe the inexorable Clotho with a quarter of a million sterling and will throw in two large mixing bowls each weighing a hundred talents of fine gold. The offer is refused, and the ghosts are finally rounded up ready to embark. They are numerous, and they carry much luggage. Charon's boat is old and leaky, and the company will submerge it unless they are stripped of their impediments. The dandy must be stripped of his good looks, his flowing hair, and his rosy cheeks; the tyrant must give up his diadem, his royal mantle, and his pride and superciliousness; the athlete must give up his lumps of flesh and his trophies; the miser must surrender his gold; Craton, his riches, his effeminacy, his luxury, his pride of birth, his funeral robes, and the inscriptions on his statues; the soldier must surrender his arms, for peace reigns in Hades. That rhetorician has a world of words to leave behind—antitheses, figures of speech, periods, and cadences—and that philosopher must leave, not only his sophisms and the claptrap of his deceitful trade, but his shameless luxury and his enormous beard. That they cut off with the ship's carpenter's axe. Having been decently stripped, the ghosts embark, all but Mycillus, the cobbler, for whom no place can be found. He is anxious to go, since life has meant nothing to him but penury, and he is tired of his old shoes, so he plunges in to swim across the Styx, and they have perforce to take him aboard. As they are shoving off, Menippus hears a cry on earth, and Hermes tells him it is the sound of funeral eulogies and dirges for some of his fellow passengers. "No one sheds a tear for you," says Hermes, "and you lie in perfect peace." "You are wrong," says Menippus. "You will shortly hear the dogs snarling over my body, and the crows flapping their wings when they assemble to bury me."

Dryden and Fénelon were Lucianists, and Defoe wrote a Lucianic satire that landed him in the pillory. It was entitled "The Shortest Way with Dissenters." In this, pretending to write as a bigoted churchman, Defoe gravely recommended that all dissenters be put to death. Dissenters, he said, were incorrigible and a perpetual menace to truth in religion. Confronted by such a proposition your bigot might say, "That is exactly right; the only thing to do with them is to kill them." Your man of more moderate views might say, "I think you are going too far, brother!" or, more probably, "I will have nothing to do with an institution which coldly recommends the slaughter of thousands of innocent people." And thus the church party would lose support, and Defoe's object would be accomplished. Swift produced the most gruesome of all satires in his "A Modest Proposal." Not only have we *Gulliver's Travels* and other Lucianic works by Swift, Arbuthnot, and Fielding, but it may be said that the periodical literature of the time, its brightness, its pugnacity, and its tendency to carry on to extremes, shows qualities unmistakably Lucianic. There is also something Lucianic in American humor. The elements of its composition are of course varied, but there is more than a thread of Lucianism in it. Consider the spectacle of Mark Twain shedding tears over the reputed grave of Adam, who was a relation of his; or, when he was examining the Egyptian mummy, his asking, "Is he dead?" The American has always, or at least traditionally, been the sort of man who not only says that the horse is seventeen feet high, but proves it. Benjamin Franklin was a lover of the hoax as such, and was, like the eighteenth-century essayists, a consistent employer of the Lucianic device. One thinks of his "Rules by which a Great Empire may be reduced to a Small One" and his "Edict of the King of Prussia." In his *Dialogue between Franklin and the Gout* he seems actually to parallel Lucian.

I am not, however, primarily interested in talking to you about the history of literature, interesting as I have always found that subject to be. I have tried to tell you that I think of many of the ancient classics as discoveries in the realm of mind, as inventions in thought, as keys by which the mystery cupboards and treasure chests of life are opened. It is not necessary that they should all be opened, and we certainly cannot open them all. Life would be richer and wiser if these keys were used, but we must perforce content ourselves with knowing what is there and with showing it like wise custodians to the few who are able to appreciate it. So far as popularity is concerned, it, in the long run, takes pretty good care of itself, and we do not have to worry ourselves too much. I have talked to you illustratively about the intellectual discoveries of an ingenious and ultimately wise man who developed methods of attack on the human weaknesses and inconsistencies of his own time, a time in some ways not too unlike our own and other times. It is one of those social and ancestral patterns that all human brains tend inevitably to form. I believe that similar studies will account for the longevity of many other ancient classics, some of which are not in the least satirical but are prized for the truths they tell us about our natures and our lives. They range all the way from the simplest folk tales to the greatest products of the race— great epics, great dramas, great novels, great treatises, great histories, and great works of religion. If we know what they are in their essence, it is possible that such knowledge will increase our faith, add to our patience, and mature our wisdom. In this area I flatter myself that scientists, philosophers, and teachers of literature have a good deal in common.

III

Hamlet and Ophelia

Hamlet IS POSSIBLY the best-known literary work in the world, and it is therefore with some assurance that you will understand me that I talk to you with some intimacy about that play. What I have learned about Shakespeare's great drama can be summed up in the statement that Hamlet is Everyman. His faults and his troubles, as well as his virtues, are merely those of all men. He is not typically a procrastinator or a pessimist; but his procrastination, his self-distrust, and his bitterness are merely those that attend the living of a human life. Many attempts have been made to explain him away by finding an hypothesis that will settle his case, but he continually pops out of his pigeonhole and again confronts us as somehow a significant example. The generality of his type therefore is the explanation of his undying popularity. I have selected for consideration a comparatively separable aspect of the great play of *Hamlet,* namely, the relation between Hamlet and Ophelia. There is a great deal to be learned from this relation, both about the play and about men and women in the world.

I should like to begin this lecture by talking to you for a few minutes about the morals of the Polonius family. These morals are well known and widely admired. Polonius in his advice to his son Laertes gives a perfect expression of his code. You will remember it. Laertes has already bade his father farewell. Polonius enters and expresses some surprise. "Aboard, aboard for shame!" he says, and on Laertes' request for "a double blessing" utters a few precepts that he would have Laertes "charácter" in his memory. "Give thy thoughts no tongue," he says, "nor any unproportioned thought his act."

[32]

"Do not dull thy palm with entertainment of each new-hatch'd, unfledg'd comrade."

> Beware of entrance into quarrel; but being in,
> Bear't that the opposed may beware of thee.

"Give every man thine ear, but few thy voice." Also "Take each man's censure, but reserve thy judgement," a statement that has always reminded me of Burns's lines in "An Epistle to a Young Friend":

> Conceal yoursel as weel's ye can
> Frae critical dissection,
> But keek though every ither man
> Wi' sharpened sly inspection.

Then Polonius would have Laertes dress well and like a gentleman, "for the apparel oft proclaims the man"—"rich not gaudy" being the idea. Then he says with weighty and convincing wisdom:

> Neither a borrower nor a lender be;
> For loan oft loses both itself and friend,
> And borrowing dulls the edge of husbandry.

My possibly frivolous imagination has always associated this with a verse in an old Princeton song:

The town is full of talent and lager beer saloons;
The boys sometimes get hard up and pawn their pantaloons;
But this thing seldom happens, the reason you can see,
We always borrow when we're short in New Jersee.

Polonius ends with the famous Renaissance motto: "to thine own self be true,"

> And it must follow, as the night the day,
> Thou canst not then be false to any man. [I, iii, 55-81]

I don't know exactly what that means, but let no man despise this code of morals, for on it rests the order of society. Socially this code is directed toward honest and thrifty conduct in business and toward prudent and profitable matrimony. And yet it is but a formal code. It lays stress on rules of conduct and not on honor and conscience. There is indeed a higher kind of ethics that includes all this and proceeds sincerely to work righteousness because it is right and to eschew evil because it is evil. Many of you will see that I am speaking of the familiar three steps in the Platonic ladder as it applies in the field of ethics, that is, the ethics of mere sensuality and selfishness, the ethics of the prudential intellect, and the ethics of spiritual intuition. Bacon was aware of this higher range of spiritual ethics and, particularly, John Milton in *Areopagitica* and elsewhere gave it full expression. It is the voluntary ethics of the freeman. Let us see if we can make clear the application of these principles to the play of *Hamlet*.

When Laertes in the same scene in which he receives his father's advice warns his sister against the attentions and intentions of Hamlet, Laertes evidently thinks that, if given the chance, Hamlet will take advantage of Ophelia's love and innocence in order to ruin her. Polonius thinks the same thing, and I fear we must attribute the same views to Ophelia herself. Now, you and I know perfectly well that Hamlet is incapable of behaving in any such way. We know that Ophelia would be perfectly safe in his hands. We know without being told that Hamlet operates according to a different and, we may say, a higher code of ethics. The whole Polonius family are on the prudential level. Polonius contrives, manipulates, and operates in terms of caution and personal advantage. He does not trust other people or believe in any ideals of abstract and complete virtue. He permits Laertes to waste his time in Paris because that is the proper thing for young noblemen to do, but not without setting a spy on to watch him. Laertes accepts the same code, as when he professes later on that he cannot accept reconciliation with Hamlet except on the advice of "certain masters of known honor." Ophelia's role in this family and this atmosphere is obedience, and she is properly and perfectly obedient. The whole family is completely conventional in its thinking; and, so far as Ophelia is concerned, she, like many other girls then and now, merely awaits matrimony. So closely is this wall of inhibitions drawn down about her that, although she undoubtedly loves Hamlet, her love is hedged in and unrealized by the ethics of her family. It might almost be said that, although she loves Hamlet, she does not know what true love demands. She lacks the confidence of love and has no philosophy of love or of herself as a person, for she has been brought up on maxims.

Let me now introduce an important principle in the interpretation of Shakespeare, and that is this: Shakespeare almost never varies from the facts he got from his sources. There are a few cases where he does so, such as the behavior of Isabella in *Measure for Measure* as compared to Cassandra in Whetstone's play; also in the tragic ending he gives to *King Lear* as compared to the plot he got from the old *King Leir*. But, in general, Shakespeare does not alter fact as he found it in his sources. There is nothing especially commendable about this. It merely means that Shakespeare and most of the writers of his age had an unshaken respect for fact, which was God's manifestation of what had happened and might happen on earth. It had simply not occurred to them that fact could be or needed to be invented. There was of course a certain amount of change, casual or particular, but outright invention of plot was a long way in the future. Perhaps there is nothing very conscious and definite in that way until one gets to Richardson and Fielding in the eighteenth century. Fact and event were to the Elizabethans the function and prerogative of God. The freedom the Elizabethans enjoyed was of a different sort, being a freedom of operation and conception and of the significance and interpretation of actual occurrence. To Shakespeare the world seemed in this way to be plastic, and he proceeded with the utmost freedom, indeed the greatest genius, in what we should call interpretation. The Poet in

Timon of Athens speaks of his own genius as operating in "a vast sea of wax."

The plot of *Hamlet* from its first appearance in the *Historia Danica* of Saxo Grammaticus varies but little through to Shakespeare's refined masterpiece. It is believed that there were certain additions to the plot of *Hamlet* by the dramatist Thomas Kyd in a version of the story now lost and usually called "the Old Hamlet." But the main features of the plot remained steadfast. Of course in interpretations and manipulations the differences are considerable, but the story remained the same it is today, namely, the story of the contest of a righteous subtlety and intelligence, on the one side, against superior evil force on the other. This has always been a main issue in the world. In the old story (and the new) Hamlet pretends to be dull of wits and little better than a beast, while he is secretly plotting a just revenge. It is his humor to speak and act in such a way that he puzzles the king and the courtiers, and by his riddling words he arouses their suspicions. This riddling quality, this taking of calculated risks, is a feature of the Hamlet story from the beginning and has constituted one of its principal charms. The usurping, adulterous, and murderous king and his henchmen are suspicious, and they make three attempts to pluck out the heart of Hamlet's mystery. These attempts, as you will see, are still the structural features of Shakespeare's play. First, two of his companions (Rosencrantz and Guildenstern in the play) attempt to gain Hamlet's confidence so that they can betray him to the king. He foils their attempts and sends them to their deaths. Secondly, a courtier (Polonius in the play) in the old story hides in Hamlet's mother's bedchamber under a heap of straw (evidently the queen's bed) in order to overhear a conversation between Hamlet and his mother, for the king and his courtiers think Hamlet will be likely to betray his secret in a conversation with her. Hamlet mounts the heap of straw and crows like a cock. He feels the courtier under his feet and, crying

out, "A rat!" stabs the courtier in the straw. Thirdly, the
king and his followers set on a bad woman to seduce Hamlet,
for they believe that under the influence of love Hamlet will
betray his secret to this treacherous courtesan. This is the
original and unattractive role of the fair Ophelia. Very un-
promising, one would say!

It will be seen that, according to the terms of the fixed plot,
Ophelia is obliged to operate against Hamlet. It is Shakespeare's handling of the motives, characters, causes, and circumstances that gives interest and eternal significance to the
relation between Hamlet and Ophelia. Shakespeare's interest
was always in good women. He did not wish to present Ophelia
as a bad woman, and one can hear him asking himself how a
good woman could have been induced to play the part that
Ophelia plays. He knew that the society of his time produced
a kind of woman who, preserving her innocence, would do
what the plot demanded. He therefore presents her as domi-
nated by her father and her father's mores, as many good girls
have been and still are. Ophelia has no mother; but strict
family discipline, a discipline both of thought and conduct,
is embodied in Polonius. Polonius is an excellent disciplina-
rian—a formal, efficient man, a close observer of detail, and a
server of his times. His mind and his morals are narrow, prudential, selfish, and tyrannical. Ophelia, since she simply does
not think for herself at all, is thus made capable of betraying
Hamlet without in the least intending to do so; indeed, of betraying him while she loves him and longs for his love. In
this use of ignorance and chance, things to which all human
beings are subject and liable, Shakespeare enters the field of
possible tragedy.

Shakespeare has elevated his story and increased its poig-
nancy and its tragic possibility by making Hamlet and Ophelia
each deeply in love with the other. There is a conflict of spiritual level between them, and they love in different ways, but
they both love truly. It is foredoomed by the plot and the

circumstances that Ophelia should betray her lover, fail him
in his need, and do these things as a consequence of her education, her situation, her training, and perhaps her nature.
Let us look at the play.

Hamlet, after the revelation of his father's ghost, is no
longer a free agent. He has had laid upon him an all-absorb-
ing duty. Nothing may be permitted to interfere with it.

> Remember thee!
> Ay, thou poor ghost, while memory holds a seat
> In this distracted globe. Remember thee!
> Yea, from the table of my memory
> I'll wipe away all trivial fond records,
> All saws of books, all forms, all pressures past,
> That youth and observation copied there,
> And thy commandment all alone shall live
> Within the book and volume of my brain,
> Unmix'd with baser matter.   [I, v, 95-104]

It will be interesting at this point to find out what Ophelia
thinks of him and thus get an idea of what sort of man Hamlet was. When he leaves her after the interview in the first
scene of the third act, she says:

> O, what a noble mind is here o'erthrown!
> The courtier's, soldier's, scholar's eye, tongue, sword;
> The expectancy and rose of the fair state,
> The glass of fashion and the mould of form,
> The observ'd of all observers, quite, quite down!
> And I, of ladies most deject and wretched,
> That suck'd the honey of his music vows,
> Now see that noble and most sovereign reason,
> Like sweet bells jangled out of tune and harsh;
> That unmatch'd form and feature of blown youth
> Blasted with ecstasy. O, woe is me,
> To have seen what I have seen, see what I see!
>   [III, i, 158-69]

Hamlet did not abandon Ophelia until he had made sev-
eral recorded efforts to find out whether or not she was on his
side. No man who has ever been in love and in trouble will

need to have it explained to him how much Hamlet needed at that time the sympathy of the woman he loved. He was in deep trouble, and he wanted to find out if she was true to him. No man has a deeper respect for wifely admonition than I have. Knowing the pigritude of men as I do, I will go so far as to say that I think a good deal of what is called "nagging" is justified and beneficial; but, if I pay a woman's board, I want her to be on my side. Ophelia herself reports an interview between them in which Hamlet spoke no words. It is a terrible thing, an ominous spectacle. She has been denying him her society and has sent back sundry tokens of love he has given her. He goes into her closet to see about it, and he weighs her in the balance and finds her wanting. She comes rushing to her father much disturbed, and he says:

> How now, Ophelia! what's the matter?
> *Oph.* Alas, my lord, I have been so affrighted!
> *Pol.* With what, in the name of God?
> *Oph.* My lord, as I was sewing in my chamber,
> Lord Hamlet, with his doublet all unbrac'd,
> No hat upon his head, his stockings foul'd,
> Ungart'red, and down-gyv'd to his ankle,
> Pale as his shirt, his knees knocking each other,
> And with a look so piteous in purport
> As if he had been loosed out of hell
> To speak of horrors,—he comes before me.

Polonius, being a practical man, first comes to a conclusion and later hears the evidence. He says:

> Mad for thy love?

And Ophelia, in words that I have always been sorry she uttered, replies:

> My lord, I do not know,
> But truly I do fear it.

In response to a demand from her father she describes the ordeal:

> He took me by the wrist and held me hard;

> Then goes he to the length of all his arm,
> And, with his other hand thus o'er his brow,
> He falls to such perusal of my face
> As he would draw it. Long stay'd he so.
> At last, a little shaking of mine arm,
> And thrice his head thus waving up and down,
> He rais'd a sigh so piteous and profound
> That it did seem to shatter all his bulk
> And end his being. That done, he lets me go;
> And with his head over his shoulder turn'd,
> He seem'd to find his way without his eyes,
> For out o' doors he went without their help,
> And, to the last, bended their light on me.
>
> [II, i, 74-102]

Most people would say, "Poor Ophelia!" but I would also say, "Poor Hamlet!" Polonius, still in the belief that "this is the very ecstasy of love," says, "Go with me, I will go seek the king."

There is the record of a second trial, this time in the form of a letter. The king has been busy hearing the report of his ambassadors to Norway, and Polonius is fuming to get his chance to tell his news. He says:

> This business is well ended.
> My liege, and madam, to expostulate
> What majesty should be, what duty is,
> Why day is day, night night, and time is time,
> Were nothing but to waste night, day, and time;
> Therefore, since brevity is the soul of wit
> And tediousness the limbs and outward flourishes,
> I will be brief. Your noble son is mad.
> Mad call I it; for, to define true madness,
> What is't but to be nothing else but mad?
> But let that go.

The queen, having heard Hamlet's madness mentioned, is impatient and says:

> More matter, with less art.
> *Pol.* Madam, I swear I use no art at all.

That he is mad 'tis true; 'tis true 'tis pity,
And pity 'tis 'tis true. A foolish figure!
But farewell it, for I will use no art.
Mad let us call him then; and now remains
That we find out the cause of this effect,
Or rather say, the cause of this defect,
For this effect defective comes by cause.
Thus it remains, and the remainder thus.
Perpend.
I have a daughter—have whilst she is mine—
Who, in her duty and obedience, mark,
Hath given me this. Now, gather and surmise.

"To the celestial and my soul's idol, the most beautified
Ophelia,"—That's an ill phrase, a vile phrase; "beautified" is a
vile phrase. But you shall hear. Thus: "In her excellent white
bosom, these."

> *Queen.* Came this from Hamlet to her?
> *Pol.* Good madam, stay a while. I will be faithful.
> "Doubt thou the stars are fire,
>   Doubt that the sun doth move,
>   Doubt truth to be a liar,
>   But never doubt I love.

O dear Ophelia, I am ill at these numbers. I have not art to
reckon my groans; but that I love thee best, O most best, believe it. Adieu.

> Thine evermore, most dear lady,
>   Whilst this machine is to him,
>   HAMLET."
>   [II, ii, 85-124]

It is a shame that this letter, which is written with Hamlet's
heart's blood, should have been read by that pompous old
donkey in open court. In spite of what Hamlet says in depre-
ciation of his skill, the letter has always in my mind associated
itself with great pieces of elemental poetry, such as Burns's

> Till a' the seas gang dry, my dear,
>   And the rocks melt wi' the sun;
> And I will luve thee still, my dear,
>   While the sands o' life shall run.

Or Wordsworth's

> No motion has she now, no force;
> She neither hears nor sees;
> Rolled round in earth's diurnal course,
> With rocks, and stones, and trees.

I am sure that Juliet would never have surrendered such a letter to the blustering of old Capulet.

I must also look with you at the Get-thee-to-a-nunnery scene, which confirms Hamlet in his rejection of Ophelia. She has suffered herself to be placed in Hamlet's way in order that the king and Polonius, who are hidden behind the arras, may overhear a conversation between her and Hamlet. She is usually given a prayerbook and placed at a prie-dieu to await his appearance. He has just uttered the To-be-or-not-to-be soliloquy, that center of indifference for himself and all the world. He sees her, and at first everything else is forgotten and she is merely the woman he loves. He addresses her with a lover's playfulness:

> Soft you now!
> The fair Ophelia! Nymph, in thy orisons
> Be all my sins rememb'red.

If she had burst into tears, if she had thrown herself into his arms, if she had fled from the stage, or done any one of half a dozen things, there would have been some hope, but she addresses him with a commonplace social greeting:

> Good my lord,
> How does your honour for this many a day?

which is equivalent to saying, "How do you do?" Hamlet is a little surprised and utters the puzzling line:

> I humbly thank you, well, well, well.

Ophelia, perhaps acting under instructions, makes another untactful move. She offers more of those unfortunate trinkets.

> My lord, I have remembrances of yours

> That I have longed long to re-deliver.
> I pray you, now receive them.

Hamlet's reply is very puzzling and is often too seriously interpreted:

> No, no.
> I never gave you aught.

Perhaps he only means, "The little things I gave you really do not matter. I am not interested in them." Then, with that simple beauty of utterance that Shakespeare gives to Ophelia, she says:

> My honour'd lord, I know right well you did,
> And with them words of so sweet breath compos'd
> As made the things more rich. Their perfume lost,
> Take these again; for to the noble mind
> Rich gifts wax poor when givers prove unkind.
> There, my lord.

Hamlet is moved by these words, and he decides to sound her out. He says:

> Ha, ha! are you honest?

The word "honest" meant, as it does now, "sincere." But it had also the social meaning of "chaste." One does not say to a lady, "Are you chaste?" and Ophelia replies with some shock:

> My lord!

Hamlet tries again and hits upon another ambiguity. He says:

> Are you fair?

He means, "Are you just or fair in your dealings with me?" But the word also meant "beautiful," and one ordinarily does not say to a lady, "Are you beautiful?" Again Ophelia shows surprise, for she again takes the social meaning of the word:

> What means your lordship?

Hamlet sees that the situation is rather hopeless and speaks trivially: "That if you be honest and fair, your honesty should admit no discourse to your beauty." Ophelia is a court lady, and she understands this and replies in kind: "Could beauty, my lord, have better commerce than with honesty?" And Hamlet goes on not ill-naturedly:

Ay, truly; for the power of beauty will sooner transform honesty from what it is to a bawd than the force of honesty can transform beauty into his likeness. This was sometime a paradox, but now the time gives it proof. I did love you once.

Oph. Indeed, my lord, you made me believe so.

Hamlet has lost hope, but he sees that Ophelia's mind is still on matrimony. Now, when a lady proposes matrimony to a man, he cannot say simply, "I'll be a brother to you." He has to explain his unwillingness, and Hamlet proceeds to do this:

You should not have believed me, for virtue cannot so inoculate our old stock but we shall relish of it. I loved you not.

Oph. I was the more deceived.

Hamlet goes on. The first thing he says has been much misunderstood. He says, "Get thee to a nunnery; why wouldst thou be a breeder of sinners?" These are plain words, but they are not brutal. I have heard actors scream out, "Get thee to a nunnery" with the accent of rage or frenzy. There were only two careers open to well-bred young women in those days—to marry or to take the veil. Hamlet is merely advising her not to marry, and he goes on to show her why he is unfit for matrimony. He accuses himself of various things. Toward the end of the speech he becomes aware that they are being spied upon by Polonius. A stage tradition has Polonius stick his head out between the curtains of the arras, but Hamlet may have heard a noise or read something from the expression of Ophelia's face. At any rate, he says, "Where is your father?" and she says, "At home, my lord." She lies to him, but what could she do? She could not say, "He is behind that arras." She is in the familiar predicament where compromise breeds falsehood.

It has seemed to me that at first Hamlet is not insane but angry: "Let the doors be shut upon him that he may play the fool nowhere but in's own house. Farewell!" He turns upon her and utters those horrid words with which we are all familiar, for in Hamlet, as in other men, loss of faith in one woman converts itself into general misogyny. Ophelia thinks he is insane. These two young people are caught in the meshes of the tragic machine of fate (III, I, 88-157).

But I must convince you of the final truth about Hamlet's love for Ophelia, and I turn to the scene at her grave. Hamlet and Horatio are in the churchyard where they have observed the digging of a grave without knowing that it was intended for Ophelia, and Hamlet has uttered his Lucianic speculations in which he shows that

> Imperial Caesar, dead and turn'd to clay,
> Might stop a hole to keep the wind away.

A funeral procession approaches, and they stand aside. Laertes' words to the churlish priest enlighten Hamlet, and he says, "What, the fair Ophelia!" The queen scatters flowers on Ophelia's bier and speaks those words that do so much to win our sympathy for that weak and sinful woman:

> I hop'd thou shouldst have been my Hamlet's wife.
> I thought thy bride-bed to have deck'd, sweet maid,
> And not to have strew'd thy grave.

Laertes, as chief mourner, makes in the old style of rhetorical grief a well-studied speech:

> O, treble woe
> Fall ten times on that cursed head
> Whose wicked deed thy most ingenious sense
> Depriv'd thee of! Hold off the earth a while,
> Till I have caught her once more in mine arms.

He leaps into Ophelia's grave and begins his principal utterance:

> Now pile your dust upon the quick and dead,
> Till of this flat a mountain you have made
> To o'ertop old Pelion, or the skyish head
> Of blue Olympus.

Hamlet, as usual, has patience only with the real thing and not with "the trappings and the suits of woe." He pushes forward the wreck of his own sincerity. He advances and cries:

> What is he whose grief
> Bears such an emphasis, whose phrase of sorrow
> Conjures the wand'ring stars and makes them stand
> Like wonder-wounded hearers. This is I,
> Hamlet, the Dane!

And he leaps into the grave. Laertes grapples with him and says:

> The devil take thy soul.

> *Ham.* Thou prayst not well.
> I prithee, take thy fingers from my throat,
> For, though I am not splenitive and rash,
> Yet have I something in me dangerous,
> Which let thy wiseness fear. Away thy hand!

The scene is scandalous, and conventionally minded readers are still shocked by it. The king cries, "Pluck them asunder." The queen says, "Hamlet, Hamlet!" They all say, "Gentlemen,—." Even Horatio says, "Good my lord, be quiet." They come out of the grave, and Hamlet's deep grief becomes vocal.

> Why, I will fight with him upon this theme
> Until my eyelids will no longer wag. . . .
> I lov'd Ophelia. Forty thousand brothers
> Could not, with all their quantity of love,
> Make up my sum. What wilt thou do for her?

And then, in words in which the weight of emotion breaks down the meter, Hamlet continues:

'Swounds, show me what thou'lt do.
Woot weep? Woot fight? Woot fast? Woot tear thyself?
Woot drink up eisel? Eat a crocodile?
I'll do't. Dost thou come here to whine?
To outface me with leaping in her grave?
Be buried quick with her, and so will I;
And, if thou prate of mountains, let them throw
Millions of acres on us, till our ground,
Singeing his pate against the burning zone,
Make Ossa like a wart! Nay, an thou'lt mouth,
I'll rant as well as thou.

The queen intervenes, and Hamlet, his passion exhausted, expostulates:

Hear you, sir,
What is the reason that you use me thus?
I loved you ever.

He gets no response, and he leaves the stage in despairing perplexity and marks his departure with words of tragic nonsense unfathomable in their pessimism:

But it is no matter.
Let Hercules himself do what he may,
The cat will mew and dog will have his day.
[V, i, 236-315]

So ends the story of Hamlet and Ophelia. It is deeply tragic, but what is a tragedy? One might say with the dictionary that a tragedy is a dramatic composition presenting on the stage a serious story in which, typically, a leading character and usually those tied in with him in the complex of life are brought to catastrophe. This may be due to weakness of character, or to fate, or to a too powerful opposition bravely resisted. In this case we might say that the tragedy is due to a failure in knowledge and wisdom. Both Hamlet and Ophelia failed to understand completely. He could not bend, and she could not adapt herself. If Juliet had been the daughter of old Polonius, and Ophelia the daughter of old

Capulet, there would have been no tragedy in either story. Can we say that tragedy is something far away in the region of history and romance? I wish we could, but we cannot. The tragic is an always present possibility of existence—in big things or in little. We are all to some degree ignorant, thoughtless, and unimaginative—all liable to mistake falsehood for truth; and all we can do is to pray God that He will enlighten our understanding, endow us with wisdom, and soften our hearts. We may leave this enigma of life with the repetition of the words of Ophelia:

"Lord, we know what we are, but know not what we may be."

And

"God, ha' mercy on his soul. And of all Christian souls, I pray God."

IV

These Juggling Fiends: On the
Meaning of Macbeth

WHEN I SPEAK of "the meaning of *Macbeth*" I am of course
well aware that there are many and various interpretations of
the import and purport, the bearings on life and the spirit,
of that great tragedy. Perhaps I ought to say "a meaning of
Macbeth," and yet I should have to add that the interpretation
I am about to give is certainly an obvious and, I think, the
original meaning of *Macbeth*. It is, as you will see, simple
and unsophisticated and is an attempt to look at the play as
it was looked at when it was put on the stage. I shall therefore ask you temporarily to put aside your superior modern
knowledge of drama and also your modernistic theories of
human conduct.

How old, let me ask you, is the concept of man as man?
I mean the quite general concept of man as Mankind, Everyman, Homo, Anthropos, and not as Priest, or King, or Con-
queror, or Servant, or Yeoman. This complete abstraction,
although old, cannot be the oldest of concepts in the general
category. One can see that in the formation of such a concept
tyrants, kings, heroes, patriarchs, and warriors must actually
have contributed to the formation of the general idea of man
in the abstract. On their careers and opinions the general
concept must have been formed. For the sake of understanding, let me put what I have just said in the form of a question:
What is the fate of man on earth? If I should stop now and
ask you this question, I should certainly get a widely varied
and most interesting set of answers, for one cannot say that
the question has grown easier of solution in the complexities
of the modern world.

[49]

To this question the Greeks made a profound answer. Theirs is the oldest answer that need now concern us. With them man's lot was cast in the middle of a great but clearly marked contest between Nemesis on the one side and Ate on the other. Nemesis was an inescapable punisher of all sins and an equalizer of the favors of Fortune, pulling down those whom Fortune placed in too high position. Ate was a goddess of malignant mischief, an inciter to folly and crime, and the personification of malignancy and falsehood. This alignment and identification of bounds was no doubt in some measure inherited, but it must have been mainly built out of the experience of the Greeks. They were a roving, acquisitive, seafaring race, surrounded by ferocious neighbors and frequenting the high road of the always treacherous Mediterranean Sea. It must have been natural for the Greeks to build a philosophy of the life of man out of instability and pure luck. Their conception of the fate of man in general fits in well with features we observe in the course of nature, such as ebb and flow, thesis and catharsis, growth and decay. As a pattern of man's life, the Greek idea will always find its application, for it is still probable to the thinking.

The other great historical abstraction I need not dwell upon at any length at all. It is the Christian concept of man as a sinner, which is in some respects in conflict with the Greek concept, although, as widely held, it was almost as fatalistic as Nemesis itself; but by its stress on compliance and voluntary obedience it offered a widening avenue of escape. At bottom it says that man is a sinner. This proposition is hard to deny, and for fifteen or sixteen hundred years it found few even tentative denials. Perhaps it is not yet adequately refuted. It found its most extensive expression in the great allegories of the Middle Ages, such as the pilgrimage of the life of man, the dance of death, and the morality play. Even in Shakespeare's day and long afterward, no concept of man's earthly and heavenly fate was more deeply rooted in men's minds than this, that man is an inevitable sinner and can achieve salvation only through the grace of God in the atonement of Christ.

Christian theology looked at the matter in this way: Man, although conceived in sin, is born in innocence. He is surrounded by home and kindred. His companions are conscience and good deeds. He acquires beauty, knowledge, strength, and discretion. Then enters a sin, let us say Gluttony or Lechery, often accompanied by Good Fellowship. This sin is the traveling salesman for the famous firm of the World, the Flesh, and the Devil, and he is a liar by profession. Man's backsliding is a destiny. The sin says, "Come with me," and mankind with singular objective predetermination goes away in company with the tempter and begins his career in the world. He no longer goes to confession, no longer says his prayers; but he acquires goods, forms a liaison with Lady Pleasure, and, to use our current phrase, has a good time. In the play of *Everyman* God sends death to summon Everyman, and Everyman finds to his surprise and sorrow that he has to meet death alone. His good deeds are too weak from neglect to go along with him. Nothing in this world will accompany him to that last fearful meeting. The important question now is, what is then his state? He seems to stand as a single, solitary individual just as he was at the beginning. All the lies he has believed and all the deceits that have been practiced on him are revealed for what they are. He has been cheated, deluded, ruined and disgraced; but he is still himself, and the light of truth has at last broken in upon him. His only value is in his immortal soul, which by an incredible mercy is precious in the sight of God. But immediately he is damned for the life he has lived, and Hell is his destination unless God and His saints intervene.

This theme in essential form appears again and again in the drama of the late Middle Ages and the Renaissance, usually, but not always, narrowed in its scope to apply to special classes of men and special situations in life. The Renaissance, however, with its current of individualization, changed the stress. It emphasized the element of responsibility, and in that change there gradually appeared the idea that character is destiny. I shall spare you the particular results of my investigation. Most morality plays of the Tudor period dealt, even when they proceeded according to the pattern of the morality play, with some special human situation already recorded in story or chronicle. A few of them did, however, present the idea of man as a representative of mankind. The conspicuous case is that of Marlowe's *Dr. Faustus,* which is a perfectly generalized morality, and, considering the way it is marked, it is absurd to think that Marlowe did not know exactly what he was doing when he wrote it. Faustus rejects, under the deceitful persuasions of the Devil, but not without a proneness to sin on his own part, all the good he has done in the past as well as all the good he might do in the future in favor of a sinful life. He rounds out a career of twenty-four years of worldliness characterized more by futility than by evil and, at the end, stands as one condemned before the judgment of God and in the clutches of Satan and his rabble. There is in *Dr. Faustus* no implemented idea of divine intercession, but the idea of salvation through intercession is as passionately and intensely present as it is in any moral play. Faustus says in his last great speech:

> See, see where Christ's blood streams in the firmament!
> One drop would save my soul—half a drop! ah, my Christ!
> Mountains and hills, come, come and fall on me,
> And hide me from the heavy wrath of God! . . .
> Ah, Pythagoras' metempsychosis! were that true,
> This soul should fly from me, and I be chang'd
> Into some brutish beast! All beasts are happy,
> For when they die,
> Their souls are soon dissolved in elements;
> But mine must live, still to be plagued in hell.
> Cursed be the parents that engendered me! . . .

O soul! be chang'd to little water-drops,
And fall into the ocean—ne'er be found!—
My God, my God, look not so stern on me!

Faustus is still the same man, still a thinker, still a voyager,
but he is ruined and condemned; but note that he has been
stripped of his delusions and that there shines upon him the
light of truth; and by virtue of this illumination it may be
said that the noblest moment of his life is the last one. This
brings his story in line with the moral play and into the realm
of the purest tragedy, and, if he had been dehumanized, this
could not be said. I wish to inquire if the same thing could
be said of Macbeth.

Shakespeare's transcendent merit is that he generalizes his
heroes, so that most of them present, not their own experiences
only, but the experience of all mankind. One sees this most
obviously in such figures as King Richard II, Hotspur, King
Henry V, Brutus, Mark Anthony, Timon, and Coriolanus.
But perhaps the perfect typicality of his heroes appears only
in Hamlet and Macbeth. It is Macbeth I wish to talk about,
and I shall resort to the play.

Macbeth was essentially a good man well regarded by his
king and his compatriots. He was a professional soldier of
great ability and matchless courage. Let us hear the Wounded
Captain:

Doubtful it stood,
As two spent swimmers that do cling together
And choke their art. The merciless Macdonwald—
Worthy to be a rebel, for to that
The multiplying villainies of nature
Do swarm upon him—from the Western Isles
Of kerns and gallowglasses is suppli'd;
And Fortune, on his damned quarrel smiling,
Show'd like a rebel's whore. But all's too weak;
For brave Macbeth—well he deserves that name—
Disdaining Fortune, with his brandish'd steel,
Which smok'd with bloody execution,
Like Valour's minion carv'd out his passage

Till he fac'd the slave;
Which ne'er shook hands, nor bade farewell to him,
Till he unseam'd him from the nave to the chaps,
And fix'd his head upon our battlements.   [I, ii, 7-23]

Macbeth was tempted by the thin delusions of the Devil, who really had and has nothing to offer but flattery and temptation bolstered up by a slight and valueless framework of fact:

Macb. Aside. Two truths are told,
As happy prologues to the swelling act
Of the imperial theme.—I thank you, gentlemen.
Aside. This supernatural soliciting
Cannot be ill, cannot be good. If ill,
Why hath it given me earnest of success,
Commencing in a truth? I'm thane of Cawdor.
If good, why do I yield to that suggestion
Whose horrid image doth unfix my hair
And make my seated heart knock at my ribs,
Against the use of nature? Present fears
Are less than horrible imaginings.
My thought, whose murder yet is but fantastical,
Shakes so my single state of man that function
Is smother'd in surmise, and nothing is
But what is not.   [I, iii, 128-42]

He has, as this passage shows, the roots of sin in his heart. His wife, who also joins the fiends against him, makes his attitude as clear as a diagram:

Yet do I fear thy nature;
It is too full o' the milk of human kindness
To catch the nearest way. Thou wouldst be great,
Art not without ambition, but without
The illness should attend it. What thou wouldst highly,
That wouldst thou holily; wouldst not play false,
And yet wouldst wrongly win. Thou'dst have, great Glamis,
That which cries, "Thus thou must do, if thou have it";
And that which rather thou dost fear to do
Than wishest should be undone. Hie thee hither
That I may pour my spirits in thine ear,

And chastise with the valour of my tongue
All that impedes thee from the golden round
Which fate and metaphysical aid doth seem
To have thee crown'd withal.   [I, v, 17-31]

At this point we must give some attention to Lady Macbeth. That she is a clever, capable, self-confident woman is
evident from the passage I have just read, as also from the
fact that she knows her husband perfectly. It is also clear
from what follows that she knows how to manage her husband. This is Kittredge's famous analysis of her attack: "You
are afraid to do it," she said. Then, "You will do it if you
love me." And, finally, "If you don't do it, I'll do it myself."
These precepts certainly mark the highway to the control of
men. But she goes further. Macbeth was a worshiper of
courage, which was at the center of his being, and she puts
before him an ideal of daring over which the world still
shudders:

> *Lady M.* What beast was't, then,
> That made you break this enterprise to me?
> When you durst do it, then you were a man;
> And, to be more than what you were, you would
> Be so much more the man. Nor time nor place
> Did then adhere, and yet you would make both.
> They have made themselves, and that their fitness now
> Does unmake you. I have given suck, and know
> How tender 'tis to love the babe that milks me;
> I would, while it was smiling in my face,
> Have pluck'd my nipple from his boneless gums
> And dash'd the brains out, had I so sworn as you
> Have done to this.
> *Macb.*   If we should fail?
>
> *Lady M.*   We fail!
>
> But screw your courage to the sticking-place,
> And we'll not fail.   [I, vii, 47-61]

Secondly, Lady Macbeth is a woman of marvelous self-control.
She stated and practiced the James-Lange theory long before

it was rediscovered. She knows that passions are felt in their expression only, and that to refuse to give them voice is to strangle them in their birth. "You do unbend your noble strength," she says, "to think so brainsickly of things." We have also the magnificent exhibition of self-control in the banqueting scene:

> This is the very painting of your fear;
> This is the air-drawn dagger which, you said,
> Led you to Duncan. O, these flaws and starts,
> Impostors to true fear, would well become
> A woman's story at a winter's fire,
> Authoriz'd by her grandam. Shame itself!
> Why do you make such faces? When all's done,
> You look but on a stool.   [III, iv, 61-68]

Macbeth enters upon his career of crime with his eyes open.

> If it were done when 'tis done, then 'twere well
> It were done quickly. If the assassination
> Could trammel up the consequence, and catch
> With his surcease success; that but this blow
> Might be the be-all and the end-all here,
> But here, upon this bank and shoal of time,
> We'ld jump the life to come. But in these cases
> We still have judgement here, that we but teach
> Bloody instructions, which, being taught, return
> To plague the inventor. This even-handed justice
> Commends the ingredients of our poison'd chalice
> To our own lips. He's here in double trust:
> First, as I am his kinsman and his subject,
> Strong both against the deed; then, as his host,
> Who should against his murderer shut the door,
> Not bear the knife myself. Besides, this Duncan
> Hath borne his faculties so meek, hath been
> So clear in his great office, that his virtues
> Will plead like angels, trumpet-tongu'd, against
> The deep damnation of his taking-off.   [I, vii, 1-20]

So also does Lady Macbeth know the significance of the sinful deed. To be sure, he knows far more about the practical consequences of the crime than she does. As a soldier, courtier, and man of the world, he ought to know more about them. But on the strictly moral side, she has as deep a sense of the sinfulness of the deed as he has, perhaps a deeper sense. In the midst of the murder she throws out that strange signum:

> Had he not resembled
> My father as he slept, I had done 't.

In quite modern terms it may be said that she had the power of shoving inconvenient and unpleasant things into her unconscious and of keeping them there—while she was awake. But when she slept they asserted themselves. Do we need the doctrines of Freud to understand this natural and familiar fact?

Lady M. Out, damned spot! out, I say!—One: two: why, then 'tis time to do't.—Hell is murky!—Fie, my lord, fie! a soldier, and afeard? What need we fear who knows it, when none can call our power to account?—Yet who would have thought the old man to have had so much blood in him?

Doct. Do you mark that?

Lady M. The thane of Fife had a wife; where is she now? —What, will these hands ne'er be clean?—No more o' that, my lord, no more o' that; you mar all with this starting.

. . . .

Here's the smell of the blood still; all the perfumes of Arabia will not sweeten this little hand. Oh, oh, oh!

. . . .

To bed, to bed! there's knocking at the gate. Come, come, come, come, give me your hand. What's done cannot be undone.—To bed, to bed, to bed!   [V, i, 39-76]

What a shame it was that Macbeth, the man who knew the laws of the land, the man inured to war, permitted this delicate creature to engage in dark contrivance and in butchery!

Here I introduce a speculation about which I am by no means sure, and I should like you to think about it. Lady Macbeth is a strong character, and her strength is a womanly strength. I have been trying to show that Macbeth is a lineal descendant of Everyman. I diffidently suggest that Lady Macbeth is a lineal descendant of Everywoman.

Macbeth, like Faustus, reaps a harvest of thorns, a devil's harvest without value or satisfaction. He is prey to suspicion and disappointment:

> To be thus is nothing;
> But to be safely thus. Our fears in Banquo
> Stick deep; and in his royalty of nature
> Reigns that which would be fear'd. . . .
>
> .   .   .   .
>   He chid the sisters
> When first they put the name of king upon me,
> And bade them speak to' him; then prophet-like
> They hail'd him father to a line of kings.
> Upon my head they plac'd a fruitless crown,
> And put a barren sceptre in my gripe,
> Thence to be wrench'd with an unlineal hand,
> No son of mine succeeding. If't be so,
> For Banquo's issue have I fil'd my mind;
> For them the gracious Duncan have I murder'd;
> Put rancours in the vessel of my peace
> Only for them; and mine eternal jewel
> Given to the common enemy of man.   [III, i, 48-69]

He inherits the contempt of honest men:

> *Len.* My former speeches have but hit your thoughts,
> Which can interpret farther; only, I say,
> Things have been strangly borne. The gracious Duncan
> Was pitied of Macbeth; marry, he was dead:
> And the right-valiant Banquo walk'd too late;
> Whom, you may say, if't please you, Fleance kill'd,
> For Fleance fled; men must not walk too late.
> Who cannot want the thought how monstrous
> It was for Malcolm and for Donalbain
> To kill their gracious father? Damned fact!
> How it did grieve Macbeth! Did he not straight
> In pious rage the two delinquents tear,
> That were the slaves of drink and thralls of sleep?
> Was not that nobly done? Ay, and wisely too;
> For 'twould have anger'd any heart alive
> To hear the men deny't.   [III, vi, 1-16]

He manifests the hardness of gratuitous and revengeful crime:

> *Enter Murderers*
> L. Macd.   What are these faces?
> l. Mur.   Where is your husband?
> L. Macd.   I hope, in no place so unsanctified
> Where such as thou mayst find him.
> l. Mur.   He's a traitor.
> Son. Thou liest, thou shag-ear'd villain!
> l. Mur.   What, you egg!
>   *Stabbing him*
>   Young fry of treachery!
> Son.   He has kill'd me, mother:
> Run away, I pray you!
>   *Exit Lady Macduff crying* "Murder!"
>   [IV, ii, 79-89]

He has the realization of failure and futility:

> My way of life
> Is fallen into the sear, the yellow leaf;
> And that which should accompany old age,
> As honour, love, obedience, troops of friends,
> I must not look to have; but in their stead,
> Curses, not loud but deep, mouth-honour, breath
> Which the poor heart would fain deny, and dare not.
>   [V, iii, 22-28]

And he suffers a bereavement he is unable to feel:

> *A cry of women within.*
> Macb.   What is that noise?
> Sey.   It is the cry of women, my good lord. *Exit.*
> Macb.   I have almost forgot the taste of fears.
> The time has been, my senses would have cool'd
> To hear a night-shriek, and my fell of hair
> Would at a dismal treatise rouse and stir
> As life were in't. I have supp'd full with horrors;
> Direness, familiar to my slaughterous thoughts,
> Cannot once start me.
>   *Re-enter Seyton.*
>   Wherefore was that cry?
> Sey.   The Queen, my lord, is dead.
> Macb. She should have died hereafter;

There would have been a time for such a word.
To-morrow, and to-morrow, and to-morrow,
Creeps in this petty pace from day to day
To the last syllable of recorded time;
And all our yesterdays have lighted fools
The way to dusty death. Out, out, brief candle!
Life's but a walking shadow, a poor player
That struts and frets his hour upon the stage
And then is heard no more. It is a tale
Told by an idiot, full of sound and fury,
Signifying nothing.   [V, v, 8-28]

Finally, by a reconsultation of his quack doctors, he receives truly diabolical assurances:

2 *App.* Be bloody, bold, and resolute; laugh to scorn
The power of man; for none of woman born
Shall harm Macbeth.   *Descends.*

.   .   .   .

3 *App.* Be lion-mettled, proud, and take no care
Who chafes, who frets, or where conspirers are.
Macbeth shall never vanquish'd be until
Great Birnam wood to high Dunsinane hill
Shall come against him.   *Descends.*
                                       [IV, i, 79-94]

These are the assurances of deceit, they are made of nothing, they vanish like thin air. They break down before him. What then is the final state of Macbeth and what will he do? In the light of what has been said I think we may be certain that he will still be Macbeth. Souls as such might not undergo corruption. Macduff comes in burning with indescribable wrong. He is the agent of both human and divine justice. As such he is irresistible.

Macd.   Turn, hell-hound, turn!
Macb. Of all men else I have avoided thee.
But get thee back; my soul is too much charg'd
With blood of thine already.
Macd.   I have no words,
My voice is in my sword, thou bloodier villain
Than terms can give thee out!
                         They fight. Alarum.

Macb.　　　Thou losest labour.
As easy mayst thou the intrenchant air
With thy keen sword impress as make me bleed.
Let fall thy blade on vulnerable crests;
I bear a charmed life, which must not yield
To one of woman born.
Macd.　　　Despair thy charm;
And let the angel whom thou still hast serv'd
Tell thee, Macduff was from his mother's womb
Untimely ripp'd.
Macb. Accursed be that tongue that tells me so,
For it hath cow'd my better part of man!
And be these juggling fiends no more believ'd
That palter with us in a double sense,
That keep the word of promise to our ear,
And break it to our hope. I'll not fight with thee.
Macd. Then yield thee, coward,
And live to be the show and gaze o' the time.
We'll have thee, as our rarer monsters are,
Painted upon a pole, and underwrit,
"Here may you see the tyrant."
Macb.　　　I will not yield,
To kiss the ground before young Malcolm's feet
And to be baited with the rabble's curse.
Though Birnam wood be come to Dunsinane,
And thou oppos'd, being of no woman born,
Yet I will try the last. Before my body
I throw my warlike shield. Lay on, Macduff,
And damn'd be him that first cries, "Hold, enough!"
　　　　　　　　　　　　　　　　　[V, viii, 3-34]

And be these juggling fiends no more believ'd
That palter with us in a double sense,
That keep the word of promise to the ear,
And break it to our hope.

With this masterly definition of evil, we see that every shred of deceit is torn away. Macbeth, now reduced to the lowest level of actuality, does the only thing he can do. He dies with his sword in his hand.

The meaning of *Macbeth* is therefore this: The Devil is a liar.

V

Burns and Lowland Scotch

ALMOST EVERYTHING that can be said about Robert Burns has already been said; and it is my firm belief in the principle of inclusiveness, in the value of range and scope of reading, that causes me to talk to you about Burns. I should like more American students and readers of literature to understand, admire, and habitually read Burns, and my purpose may therefore be described as operative, or, if you like, as pedagogical. I am an American teacher of literature, and, after all these years, my hand, like that of the dyer, is subdued into that in which it works. I should not, however, lecture to you on Burns if I did not believe that he is a very great poet and that, of all poets, he is perhaps the greatest poet of ordinary life. His beauty, his insight, his wisdom are of the sort that come home to the business and bosoms of ordinary men and women. He does that now to a surprising extent, but not so greatly as he easily might, since his spirit and finer meaning are often missed, and his language is often an unnecessary barrier.

Burns spoke and wrote and mingled harmoniously together two languages—English and Lowland Scotch. The English we can handle, and the Lowland Scotch need give us very little trouble. Lowland Scotch is the lineal descendant of ancient Northumbrian, the northernmost dialect of the Anglo-Saxon conquerors. Lowland Scotch is by far the most important of English dialects, and in it, or in a mixture of it with English, have appeared some of the most significant and most representative things that the Anglo-Saxon race has recorded in its literature. In Lowland Scotch is an ancient literature, and perhaps its heyday was more than four hundred years ago. The north country is the land of virility, industry, and good sense, and neither Great Britain nor any of its outspreadings, including the United States of America, would have the virtues and powers they possess without Scotland and the north country.

I pass over the roll of great names in the history of Scottish literature and merely ask you to remember that the educated Scot has always known English as well as Scotch, especially since the adoption in Scotland after the Reformation of the King James version of the Bible, and that much of the greatest Scottish literature appears in normal and often forceful English. Scottish intellect, temperament, character, and sentiment appear in English in Hume, Scott, Carlyle, Stevenson, Barrie, Lord Tweedsmuir, and many others. This part of Scottish literature is a firmly held possession, but works and parts of works written in Lowland Scotch are less firmly held and yet are necessary for complete comprehension and enjoyment of literary Scotland. Even within the last generation there has occurred, although few people outside Scotland know it, a most interesting renascence of Scottish literature. In so far as it appears in Gaelic, the Celtic language of the Highlands, in poets like Duncan Ban MacIntyre, Ewen Maclachlan, Allan MacDougall, Alexander Mackinnon, John MacLean, Donald MacLeod, Angus Fletcher, Allan MacIntyre, and Evan Mac-Coll, it has only indirect significance, since we are dependent on translations—often bad ones. Gaelic is to us a completely foreign language, which is said to involve special and serious difficulties; but with Lowland Scotch there are no such difficulties, and some of the newer poets in Lowland Scotch deserve a degree of attention they are not getting. I refer to such poets as A. D. Mackie, William Soutar, Marion Angus, Helen Cruickshank, Hugh MacDiarmid, and Alexander Gray. It is not, however, my intention to talk about them, since from my point of view they are readily accessible.

Lowland Scotch itself is a vast dialect of English, and within

the area of Lowland Scotch there are a large number of local
and regional manners of speech. I am disposed, for the immediate purpose of this lecture, to place these minor dialects
at a discount, although I recognize that for truer and finer
effects they are necessary. My point is that, for the reading
and enjoyment of Burns and other Lowland Scotch writers,
local dialects may, within limits, be disregarded. Burns himself did not write his Ayrshire dialect with any great consistency
or purity, and with him there began or continued a sort of
current Lowland Scotch freely mingled with English that has
become more and more a kind of linguistic coin of the realm.
Change in this matter has been very rapid during the last
fifty years, and it is not unusual to hear older Scottish people
lament the displacement of their native Doric with a sort of
generally current Lowland Scotch speech, inferior to the older
forms, no doubt, but nevertheless most convenient. What is
happening is perhaps analogous to the formation of a literary
language in the midst of a welter of dialects such as that which
came about through the domination of the Midland dialect
of London in the late Middle Ages and in early modern times.
It would be better if there were one controlling influence in
Lowland Scotch. As it is, the dialects of Burns and other later
writers of Lowland Scotch have been slowly unifying in-
fluences.

When I begin to speak of the Lowland Scottish language,
you will therefore be prepared for a certain vagueness in the
subject and a certain wide latitude in the choice of both words
and forms. You will remember that educated Scottish people,
and most of the Scotch are educated people, have spoken and
written standard English time out of mind. To be sure, they
have spoken it in their own way and have pronounced their
English with a clarity that equals or surpasses the English in the
utterance of consonants and the Americans in the utterance
of vowels. Their English is perhaps rather lower pitched than
that of the English themselves, and certainly than that of the

Americans. Scottish English is possibly a trifle slower than American English, and certainly much slower than the English of the English. Scotch seems to be level like American English and does not range through the great gamut of inflection that characterizes English as spoken in England. More than half the battle is won when one learns to read Burns and other writers of Lowland Scotch in the Scottish manner of speaking English, without any reference to dialect at all. For more than half of Burns's words are English words and were used as such by him, but they need to be uttered in the clear Scottish way in which he uttered them. To learn to do this is largely a matter of imitation and comes from association with Scottish people. The same thing may be said of learning the characteristic Scottish inflections, which tend, one might say, to the vein of understatement. These things may, however, be left to time and opportunity.

I am not urging great effort or presenting a perfectionist point of view. I am merely seeking to reassure and encourage you, my pupils and those who may read this lecture, by saying that to learn to read Burns acceptably is no very difficult matter. The Scotch themselves, particularly the older Scotch, are firmly convinced that no speaker of standard English, whether English, American, or Colonial, can possibly read and understand the Scottish poems of Robert Burns; and from the point of view of complete adequacy and impeccable skill they are no doubt right. But I am not willing to surrender one of the world's great poets to their not too zealous ministrations. The Scotch seem to take a sort of pleasure in being misunderstood, and they are very patient about it. The consciousness that for centuries they have been man for man the best educated people in the world, their frank recognition of their undoubted competency, and their clear knowledge, not only of what they have amounted to in the modern world, but of what they still amount to, have given them a pride in being and in doing that has made mere reputation a trivial matter.

Consider the infinite patience of a race that can bear with such indifference the thousands of banal music-hall jokes about the parsimony of the Scotch. But I repeat that I am not willing for the Scotch to enjoy a monopoly of Robert Burns and other great writers of Lowland Scotch.

I have some slight claims in this matter, easily brushed aside. I am the son of a Scotchman, and I heard from earliest infancy both Lowland Scotch and excellent English as spoken by the Scotch. I am not, however, proud or self-conceited, and, if there is any Scottish person present, I apologize for my performance and consent to have myself classified as at best a near-Scotchman. I have explained my motives.

Burns's spelling of Lowland Scotch is the conventional spelling he inherited from earlier Scottish poets, such as Ramsay and Fergusson, and his spelling is by no means a safe guide. One needs to learn a little Scotch, and in a surprising way acceptable forms, though with some neglect of the text, will establish themselves. I have already spoken of the Scottish manner of utterance, even when the speaker is speaking the purest of pure English, and have said that this was of prime importance in the reading of Burns; also that to learn it is a matter of observation and imitation. Everybody knows for example, that the Scotchman rolls or trills his *r*'s, and this is true. It is also true that it is hard for us who have been brought up in the South to remember this and execute it. I do not mind confessing that the failure to roll my *r*'s is the chief weakness in my own speaking of Scotch. I confess, in a cowardly fashion, that I resort to suggestion rather than to precise and unflinching performance. The point of this matter is that Burns's English poems, not often praised, are greatly vitalized by being read as a Scot would read them. For another example, one should also remember the careful use in Lowland Scotch of what is called the broad *a*. This is essential, for the Scottish *a* of this type is extremely and unvaryingly broad. Hardly less so is the fact that, whereas in English, particularly American English, short *o* has taken on an *ah*-sound, Lowland Scotch has retained a genuine short *o*. Contrast the current pronunciation of "God" with the Scottish pronunciation, which is like g-a-w-d, only much shorter. There are also cases in which the transition of long open *o* to long close *o* has not been carried through in English and has been in Scotch; the word "broad" in Scotch rhymes with "road." The long close *o* of early English developed into an *oo*-sound, but this in English has often been relaxed. I am sure you have noticed the difference in sound between f-o-o-t and b-o-o-t. In the word "foot" this sound has been, as they say, relaxed in English. The Scotchman has not consented to the relaxation, so that "foot" and other words of the kind rhyme with "boot." Also in the transition of long *u* to *ow* in such words as "house" the Scotchman has hung on rather stubbornly to the older sound. Even when he conforms to the English usage, there is a suggestion of a rounded higher sound in his utterance of words like "house" and "louse" and "mouse." All of these matters pertain to what we may call the Scottish manner of speaking English.

The Lowland Scotch that Burns wrote was not always the dialect that he must have spoken, although his language is prevailingly the Ayrshire dialect. I think we may do, with of course certain inaccuracies and inconsistencies, somewhat the same thing the Scotch themselves do. They do not, when they read or recite Burns, reproduce the Ayrshire dialect. They simply translate Burns into their own dialects, whether that of Strathearn, Clydesdale, or Fife, and proceed to read, sing, and enjoy their great national poet without let or hindrance. We may, I think, do somewhat the same thing, for we have a right to Burns just as the Scotch have a right to Shakespeare and Milton.

The handling of Scottish consonants offers little difficulty, although it is well to know which ones of them are unstable and which ones of them have differing English equivalents. The Scottish language is rather more heavily aspirated than is standard English, and has two aspirates of its own: *ch* or *gh* after *a, o,* and *u,* as in the familiar word "loch," and *ch* or *gh* after *e, i,* and *y,* as in the simple sentence, "It's a braw, bright, moonlight night the night." Although for practical purposes the spelling usually takes care of the matter, it is well to know also something about those consonants in Scotch that have been lost or, if they appear in a text, are unstable. For example, *d* tends to disappear after *n.* "Mind" becomes "min'," and "handle," "hanel." *T* goes out after *k,* so that "act" becomes "ak"; *l* disappears after the *aw*-sound and the *oo*-sound, so that "all" becomes "a" (pronounced *aw*), and "wool" becomes "woo' " or by another rule "oo"; *v* is an unstable letter, and one has "hae" for "have" and "e'en" for "even"; *f* disappears after *l,* as in "himsel' "; initial *w* is uncertain; and the *y*-sound needs to be watched like a hawk. In this matter we shall go no further than to say that "nature" becomes "natur' "; but this does not get us far, for "potatoes" are "taties" when they are not called "spuds." One thing more is imperative: there is no final *g* in Lowland Scotch for the present participle and the verbal noun. Not "singing and dancing," but "singin' and dancin' " is Scotch.

In addition to what has already been said about Lowland Scotch vowels, one might add that *a* both short and long is always of the Italian kind, so that there is a trap for English speakers in such words as "man" and "that," and the treatment of these simple and familiar words is important for the total effect. Short *e* is a little longer in Lowland Scotch than in English, and the diphthong *ai* is very pronounced, so that when the Scotsman says "ay" meaning "yes," his assent seems very cordial. Short vowels in Lowland Scotch, particularly in unaccented syllables, are a law unto themselves and vary in pronunciation from dialect to dialect. In Burns they seem to rhyme as the poet pleases.

There are differences in accent, too, that sometimes disturb the meter and cause other minor trouble. One must be prepared for April', envy', mischief', com' mittee, and comfort'- able. One who tries to speak Scotch should also avoid being ungrammatical. For example, "no" means "not," as in "I'm no goin' there." "Nae" means "no," as in "There's nae luck about the house." It is shocking to hear these common words misused. But these are relatively small matters that a little correct memorizing will quickly set right, while, at the same time, it teaches modulation, rhythm, and spirit.

I should like now to read a few passages from Burns and to comment on them briefly from the point of view of utterance and meaning. The first is from "An Epistle to John Lapraik, an old Scottish Bard."

> I am nae poet, in a sense,
> But just a Rhymer like, by chance,
> And hae to learning nae pretence
>   Yet, what the matter?
> When'er my Muse does on me glance,
>   I jingle at her.

> Your critic-folk may cock their nose,
> And say, "How can you e'er propose,
> You wha ken hardly verse frae prose,
>   To mak a sang?"
> But by your leave, my learned foes,
>   Ye're maybe wrang.

> What's a' your jargon o' the schools,
> Your Latin names for horns an' stools;
> If honest nature made you fools,
>   What sairs your grammars?
> Ye'd better ta'en up spades and shools,
>   Or knappin-hammers.

> A set o' dull conceited hashes,
> Confuse their brains in college classes!
> They gang in stirks, and come out asses,
>   Plain truth to speak;

> An' syne they think to climb Parnassus
>   By dint o' Greek!

> Gie me ae spark o' Nature's fire,
> That's a' the learning I desire;
> Then, tho' I drudge thro' dub an' mire
>   At pleugh or cart, .
> My Muse, though hamely in attire,
>   May touch the heart.

You will note that this epistle is a youthful utterance of
Burns, very manly, a trifle pertinaceous, and somewhat self-
conscious. The spelling is mainly English, and yet the tone
and some of the language is very Scottish. The question is
how far are we to read this as if it were pure Scotch. One
may safely follow the spelling and pronounce the words as
they come, and yet perhaps one ought to notice that the varying pronunciation of short vowels enables Burns to rhyme
"sense," "chance," "pretence," and "glance" without much, if
any, difference in sound. Note also that "hashes" (pronounced
"hasses") rhymes with "asses" and "classes" and that, as Burns
would have uttered it, "Parnassus" rhymes perfectly enough
with the other words. It must be that the final *us* of "Parnassus" was not felt as such, but fitted in with the ordinary
plurals in *es*. It is also impossible that Burns should have
pronounced "cart" as we do in English, even granting him a
trilled *r*. Lowland Scotch has a genuine double *t*, and therefore probably Burns did not say "matter" as we do, but
"mat-ter." Note also the use of "nae" for "no," "hae" for
"have," "wha" for "who," "shools" for "shovels," "ae" for
"one," and "pleugh" for "plow." The poem turns out to be
very Scotch, although the spelling is English enough. One
can, however, get without much linguistic effort a lively impression of this proud young rustic poet.

Let me now read you a poem so broadly Scotch that it is an
impertinence for any Southron to attempt it. It is called "To
a Haggis." Burns probably said, "Tae a Haggis."

Fair fa' your honest, sonsie face,
Great chieftain o' the puddin-race!
Aboon them a' ye tak your place,
      Painch, tripe, or thairm:
Weel are ye wordy o' a grace
      As lang's my arm.

The groaning trencher there ye fill,
Your hurdies like a distant hill,
Your pin wad help to mend a mill
      In time o' need,
While thro' your pores the dews distil
      Like amber bead.

His knife see rustic labour dight,
An' cut you up wi' ready slight,
Trenching your gushing entrails bright
      Like onie ditch;
And then, O what a glorious sight,
      Warm-reekin, rich!

Then, horn for horn, they stretch **an' strive**,
Deil tak the hindmost, on they drive,
Till a' their well-swall'd kytes belyve
      Are bent like drums;
Then auld guidman, maist like to rive,
      Bethankit hums.

Is there that o'er his French ragout,
Or olio that wad staw a sow,
Or fricassee wad make her spew
      Wi' perfect sconner,
Looks down wi' sneering, scornful view
      On sic a dinner!

Poor devil! see him owre his trash,
As feckless as a wither'd rash,
His spindle shank a guid whip-lash,
      His nieve a nit:
Thro' bloody flood or field to dash,
      O how unfit!

But mark the rustic haggis-fed,
The tremblin' earth resounds his tread,

Clap in his walie nieve a blade,
      He'll mak it whissle;
An' legs, an' arms, an' heads will sned,
      Like taps o' thistle.

Ye Pow'rs, wha mak mankind your care,
And dish them out their bill o' fare,
Auld Scotland wants nae skinking ware
      That jaups in luggies;
But, if ye wish her gratefu' prayer,
      Gie her a Haggis!

Although there is a good deal of English spelling in this poem, one who knows Lowland Scotch may go the limit. He may say "chiftn," "groanin," "men'," "dicht" and "slicht," "sneerin," "pair deevil," "resoons," and "mankin'." "To a Haggis" is one of the simplest of poems, and the chief difficulty, if there is a difficulty, is with the meanings of old Scotch words. You will note that Burns calmly rhymes "sconner" and "dinner," and "luggies" and "Haggis." To pronounce the exclamation "O" in an English way spoils the poem; it must be uttered "Och!"

Let us look finally at two little poems. Both are very simple and very beautiful.

John Anderson my jo, John,
      When we were first acquent,
Your locks were like the raven,
      And your bonie brow was brent;
But now your brow is beld, John,
      Your locks are like the snaw;
But blessings on your frosty pow,
      John Anderson my jo.

John Anderson my jo, John,
      We clamb the hill thegither;
And monie a canty day, John,
      We've had wi' ane anither:
Now we maun totter down, John,
      But hand in hand we'll go,

And sleep thegither at the foot,
John Anderson my jo.

There are many choices in this poem from dialect to dialect, and it makes no great difference within limits what choices we make. We can follow Burns's spelling, or we can say "broo," and "noo." We can say "bonie" or "bonny," "ane" or "yin," or "maun" or "mun." We can even say "han' " instead of "hand," and we can say "foot" or "fit," as we please.

The same freedom is in others of Burns's great songs, including "Auld Lang Syne." For example, consider this lyric that Burns wrote on his deathbed in honor of the neighbor girl who had soothed his sufferings:

> O, wert thou in the cauld blast,
>   On yonder lea, on yonder lea,
> My plaidie to the angry airt,
>   I'd shelter thee, I'd shelter thee.
> Or did misfortune's bitter storms
>   Around thee blaw, around thee blaw,
> Thy bield should be my bosom,
>   To share it a', to share it a'.
>
> Or were I in the wildest waste,
>   Of earth and air, of earth and air,
> The desart were a paradise,
>   If thou wert there, if thou wert there.
> Or were I monarch of the globe,
>   Wi' thee to reign, wi' thee to reign,
> The only jewel in my crown
>   Wad be my queen, wad be my queen.

As I remarked, nearly everything that can be said about Burns has already been said, but there are a few things I wish to say about him, not because they are new, but because I wish to say them. Unless one wishes to become historical, linguistic, or antiquarian, one has the impossible task of determining the universal. Burns was a universal genius like Shakespeare, and even to present the quality of these poets schematically is at once an unconvincing and an overwhelming task. To a remarkable degree Burns epitomizes humanity, and, if one is willing to forego censoriousness, it must be acknowledged that he embodied and expressed humanity at its best. He had that just and honest estimate of himself that we dignify with the name of self-respect. He acknowledged his possession of his full share of the faults, weaknesses, and even vices of humanity. He did not, however, glory in these things, but kept his mind level. It is probable that, for the sake of reproving hypocrisy, he may on occasion have flaunted his transgressions, for, like all men, he had in him a modicum of recklessness; but nobody can say he lacked a sense of humble repentance and did not aspire to and diligently practice righteousness and the service of God. So much so that it may be said of him, as of almost no other poet, that he was truly and devotedly on the right side of things. He had also a sense of his own class and its value, and he shattered the idle pretense that greatness and ability are matters of class. In no man has ever been realized more vividly the truth of the paradox that all men are equal in the sight of God.

Along with his strong, but not distorted, sense of his own individuality Burns effected a union with humanity like that of Shakespeare, Cervantes, and Dickens. No man knew better than Burns that men are far more alike than they are different, and no man ever filled out and completed an individuality more richly with the traits of humankind. This appeared in him in a sympathy almost divine in its all-embracing quality. Carlyle made some such statement as this about Burns, which I read many years ago, and I remember still two of his illustrations. One was from "A Winter Night," which expresses Burns's feeling for the creatures that suffer from the storm:

> List'ning the doors an' winnocks rattle,
> I thought me on the owrie cattle,
> Or silly sheep, wha bide this brattle
>   O' winter war,

And through the drift, deep-lairing, sprattle,
　　Beneath a scaur.

　　Ilk happing bird, wee, helpless thing!
That, in the merry months o' spring,
Delighted me to hear thee sing,
　　　　What comes o' thee?
Whare wilt thou cow'r thy chittering wing
　　And close thy e'e?

But Burns's sympathy does not stop with these good creatures;
it goes on to bad creatures:

　　E'en you on murd'ring errands toil'd,
Lone from your savage homes exil'd,
The blood-stain'd roost, and sheep-cote spoil'd
　　　　My heart forgets,
While pityless the tempest wild
　　Sore on you beats.

Burns, said Carlyle, could not hate the Devil with strict ortho-
doxy, so that he closes his famous tirade, "Address to the Deil,"
with this stanza:

　　But, fare you weel, auld Nickie-ben!
O wad ye tak a thought an' men'!
Ye aiblins might—I dinna ken—
　　　　Still hae a stake:
I'm wae to think upo' yon den,
　　E'en for your sake!

One can see how this sympathy came about in the life and
career of Robert Burns, but alas! one cannot see why. I like
to recount the simple story of Burns's life, because it seems to
me to be a miracle, not of the showy kind that make their way
into martyrologies, but a miracle of the commonplace. It will
not impress you, and, if you lived such a life, it might not make
a poet of you. Burns was born in a thatched cottage that
stands a stone's throw from the Brig o' Doon in the village of
Alloway two miles south of Ayr. When he was seven his
father leased Mt. Oliphant, a poor little farm of seventy acres

four miles from Ayr.   There was insufficient capital to stock
the farm, and the enterprise was hard sledding from the first.
When Robert was eighteen the family moved to Lochlea, a
rather better farm.   These places somehow made Robert Burns
a poet.   I have walked over both places and have wondered
how they did it.   In those barren fields, it seems, there were a
daisy, a field mouse, a laverock, and a ewe named Mailie.   They
were important agents, and one wonders if they were special.
Or, to put it another way, one wonders if God has ceased to
speak to boys on farms.   Just how Robert Burns got the sub-
stantial education he possessed one does not know.   He went
to school very little, and I think he must have taken his education into his own hands; and that too is not a bad idea.   There
were other enterprises, all more or less disastrous.   The Burns
family worked hard.   Burns always worked hard.   Burns tried
to save the situation, but matters came to an issue, as matters
have a way of doing.

The year 1786 was a crisis year.   Burns was in disgrace because of his affair with Jean Armour, and he decided to emi-
grate to the West Indies.   He had written a good many poems
that were admired among his friends, and, in order to raise
money for his voyage, he had some of them printed by a printer
in Kilmarnock—the Kilmarnock edition is now worth its
weight in precious stones.   From that time on Burns was a
famous man, was much admired and sought after, and acquired
ideas of himself as a person of more elevated social station.
It is, however, disappointing, although in general circumstances not too surprising, how little Burns got from his fame.
Very little was done that might contribute to his welfare.   After
three and one-half unprofitable years at a farm called Ellisland
on the Nith above Dumfries, Burns settled in that city for the
rest of his life, about five years, and earned his living as a
gauger of spirituous liquors.   It is said that, as he rode on his
horse from stillhouse to stillhouse, he sawed out old tunes on

his fiddle and set words to them, some of them immortal lyrics. His coming was watched for in towns and was the occasion of conviviality. This matter has, however, been exaggerated and distorted. Burns was a man of the world, and it is on record that he attended to business and wrote much poetry on the side. It was said by pious hypocrites of the kind Burns hated that he died from drink, but it is doubtful if he drank to excess. It takes a lot of whisky to kill a Scotchman. Burns died of tuberculosis of the lungs on July 21, 1796. Tuberculosis is no respecter of persons, and let us, you and I, reject forever this dismal falsehood.

VI

An Ethical Distinction by John Milton

IN THIS LECTURE stress will be put not so much on standards of
conduct, although they are of course taken for granted, as on
ethics regarded as a body of obligations and duties. Specifically it will call attention to a distinction between a group of
obligations that an individual may be said to owe to himself
and a group that an individual may be said to owe to his
fellow men. The *Nichomachean Ethics* of Aristotle continued
in the *Politics* may be said roughly to devote itself to the education or training of the individual for the exercise of both
these kinds of duty for the purpose of achieving happiness, and
the distinction between the kinds referred to is readily de-
ducible from Aristotle's work as a whole and especially from
books V, IX, and X of the *Ethics*. This distinction seems to
belong to Christian morals, for the New Testament is full of it.
I cannot find, however, that the distinction as such has any-
where been emphasized or exploited by philosophers or theo-
logians. This is a statement of simple fact as regards my own
knowledge, but in so vast a field as that of ethics one cannot
speak with any certainty when one says that the distinction
itself has not been observed and studied.

It becomes me as a nonprofessional worker in this field to
say that I do not mean to enter into the matter of origins or
of fundamental ethical values. I shall therefore put aside such
basal theories as those of conscience, intuition, utilitarianism,
and empiricism; as also questions of absolute and relative good
and other central criteria of ethical behavior. This limitation
is due to a natural desire on my part to avoid getting, as I no
doubt quickly should, beyond my depth.

The distinction between the duties one owes to oneself and

the duties one owes to one's neighbors is certainly well known, but I have been able to find no very adequate statement of it except in Milton's *De doctrina Christiana,* Book I, chapters viii-xvi. I follow Bishop Sumner's translation as republished in Patterson's *Student's Milton.*

Before, however, I attempt to give a brief analysis of Milton's treatment of ethics, let me say something about Milton's position as an authority on the subject. Milton seems to have no standing as a writer on moral philosophy like that of his contemporaries Hobbes, More, and Cudworth. He is never mentioned by general historians of ethics; and writers on Christian ethics give him rather summary treatment. Thomas Cuming Hall, for example, in his *History of Ethics within Organized Christianity* (New York, 1910), gives a brief account (pp. 435-37) of Milton as the exponent of the ethics of Independency, or rather he pretends to do so and does not. He says Milton thought he was drawing his ethics from Scriptures, but was really following Aristotle and Cicero. Milton's ethics, he says, is merely Aristotelian scholasticism in a scriptural framework. Hall is certainly wrong, but, if he were right, he might better have said that Milton's ethics is Aristotelian scholasticism drowned in Scripture, since *De doctrina Christiana* contains seven thousand chapter and verse citations from the Bible, many of them accompanied by quotation. Hall misses Milton's point in general and in particular and gives a muddled account of Milton's teachings. Milton's theological position has, on the other hand, been well studied. Both Arthur Sewell's *A Study of Milton's Christian Doctrine* (London, 1939) and Albert J. Th. Eisenring's *Milton's De doctrina Christiana* (Fribourg, Switzerland, 1946) pass over Milton's ethical doctrines apparently as a matter of no consequence. The same thing may be said with more excuse of a number of other books and articles.

There is, however, a good deal of literary appreciation of Milton's moral teachings. It is widely scattered, and I have found no systematic study of either content or application. Milton's biographers have done best, and of these no one seems to have gone much beyond Masson. It has been important to consider Milton as an antitrinitarian or as an opponent of various theological dogmas. It has not seemed so important to know what this great man thought about human conduct. But, even so, one can understand how critics might look on the substance of Milton's teachings as merely a restatement of familiar moral laws or mistake them for scholastic precepts. What surprises me and makes me uneasy is that nobody seems to have seen the significance of Milton's grand division of his subject and the importance of the field of thought that it opens up before us. It will be quickly seen that it affords a basis for his insistence on the free or voluntary nature of all true morality.

Milton (Bk. I, ch. viii), having dealt with man's duty toward God, considers the general virtues belonging to our duties as men. The general virtues, he says, are love and righteousness. These he places in a central position and recognizes in each a dual aspect. Each man owes the duty of love to himself and also to his neighbor; likewise his righteousness is a due he must render both to himself and to his neighbor. We are told that righteousness toward ourselves consists in a proper exercise of self-government.

Milton next takes up as a special class (ch. ix) the virtues connected with the duties of man toward himself. These he enumerates as temperance, a virtue that prescribes bounds to bodily gratification; secondly, sobriety, which, allied with watchfulness, consists in abstinence from immoderate eating and drinking; thirdly, chastity, which consists in temperance (used here as an inclusive word) as regards the lusts of the flesh; its opposites are effeminacy as well as all sorts of sexual vice. Negations of these virtues, he declares, are to be rated in the first instance as offenses against ourselves. In the fourth place Milton places modesty, and under immodesty he would include obscenity of language and misbehavior in reference to sex or person. Fifthly, comes decency, which, on the one side, applies to dress and decorum and, on the other, to moderation in the enjoyment of personal possessions. Milton follows these with contentment, frugality, and industry. The last two explain themselves, but he says interestingly about contentment that man should avoid overanxiety with reference to the necessities of life and should also avoid covetousness and a disposition to complain against the wisdom of God. Liberality, in the paragraph which follows, is carefully and suggestively analyzed. Liberality is to be associated with lowliness of mind, and over against it is placed arrogance, boasting, a crafty or hypocritical extenuation of one's own shortcomings, and a disposition to glory in iniquity and misdeeds. Finally, under magnanimity Milton subsumes, as does Aristotle, all those things that pertain to our own dignity rightly understood. With magnanimity he associates what we might call righteous indignation and declares that opposed to magnanimity are an overambitious spirit, pride, and pusillanimity. If Milton is right in saying that these are duties that a man owes to himself, certain things, as we shall see, inevitably follow.

As secondary virtues in this group, Milton discusses (ch. x) fortitude and patience. It is not clear why he regards them as secondary, but they too are said to occupy a middle position.

The duties a man owes to his neighbor (ch. xi-xii) turn out to be a relatively simple and easy group. Charity is described in familiar words as consisting of love toward our neighbor as toward ourselves. Love toward our neighbor, which is not clearly discriminated from charity, is either absolute or reciprocal. In its absolute aspect it takes the form of humanity, a quality well understood from its opposites, which are inhumanity, unadvised humanity, and excessive humanity. With humanity Milton quite properly associates good will and compassion. These three, humanity, good will, and compassion, are absolutes. Under reciprocal love he would place

brotherly love, Christian love, and friendship. As special virtues or duties a man owes to his neighbor, Milton lists innocence or the doing of voluntary injury to no one, meekness or
not offering or taking unwarranted offense, placability or a
readiness to forgive injuries, and a fine moral concept called
honor that would call on us to respect all the honorable feelings of our neighbors. Another chapter (xiii), which we need
not go into in detail, considers our deportment toward our
neighbors and amplifies most interestingly the general subject
of veracity. This part of the treatise is highly detailed as if
meant to serve as a particular guide in the situations and conditions of practical life. There is nothing childish or moralis-
tic about Milton's thinking or his words. He discusses sim-
plicity, faithfulness, gravity, taciturnity, courteousness, ur-
banity, freedom of speech, integrity, abstinence, commutative
justice, moderation, beneficence, and family duties. Finally,
there is discussion of private duties, such as almsgiving and
hospitality, and of public duties, such as respect for law, the
duties laid on the citizen by war, and duties pertaining to the
church.

This description will give an idea of the nature and scope
of Milton's partition of duties and their accompanying virtues. He himself draws no inference, but certain inferences
may nevertheless be drawn. We may see from even so brief an
exposition as that given above that the partition is essentially
sound. It is evident in the first place that to Milton the
achievement of goodness in human life means being something
virtuous rather than doing something virtuous. It is also immediately apparent that Milton's ethical thinking, his doctrine
of free or voluntary morality, is in line with his distinction.
His doctrine is the cradle of liberty within the law, and he
asserts it in unmistakable terms again and again—in his writing and in his life. Perhaps the clearest and most delightful
illustration is a familiar paragraph from *Areopagitica:*

"As therefore the state of man now is; what wisdom can

there be to choose, what continence to forbear, without knowledge of evil? He that can apprehend and consider vice with all her baits and seeming pleasures, and yet abstain, and yet distinguish, and yet prefer that which is truly better, he is the true wayfaring Christian. I cannot praise a fugitive and cloistered virtue unexercised and unbreathed, that never sallies out and sees her adversary, but slinks out of the race, where that immortal garland is to be run for, not without dust and heat. Assuredly we bring not innocence into the world, we bring impurity much rather; that which purifies us is trial, and trial is by what is contrary. That virtue therefore which is but a youngling in the contemplation of evil, and knows not the utmost that vice promises to her followers, and rejects it, is but a blank virtue, not a pure; her whiteness is but an excremental whiteness; which was the reason why our sage and serious poet Spenser, (whom I dare be known to think a better teacher than Scotus or Aquinas,) describing true temperance under the person of Guion, brings him in with his palmer, through the cave of Mammon, and the bower of earthly bliss, that he might see and know, and yet abstain."

Another inference, not made by Milton, is very important in what might be considered the field of operation. With reference to the duties a man owes to himself—temperance, sobriety, chastity, modesty, decency, contentment, frugality, industry, liberality, and magnanimity—it may well occur to any man that there is a good deal to do in his own shop before he goes out and begins the saving of his neighbors. Unless I am very much mistaken, we often regard the virtues enumerated as things we owe to our family, our community, our country, or our fellow men. Of this I say as politely as I can that it is nonsense. If we get it clearly in mind that we owe these duties to ourselves, and that the benefit of them solely and immediately accrues to us, it will make us less obtrusive in trying to reform the morals of other people. We say, "I am holier than thou," when we should say, "I am look-

ing after myself better than thou art looking after thyself,"
which is not a winsome thing to say. This means also that,
in the large area covered by these private virtues, reforming
the world is for the single separate individual normally an
impossibility. It follows that, if the world permits us to assist
it in reforming itself, we should not think of ourselves as conferring a favor on the world, but should really be very much
obliged. The world must reform itself, and we are mainly
limited to the less glorious task of reforming ourselves. In that
enterprise we have a great deal to do, but there is yet some
chance to succeed, whereas in the other enterprise, that of
reforming the world, the odds are naturally against us, for this
reconstitution of ourselves is our particular business, our own
affair; just as *ex hypothesi* the way in which other people do
their duty to themselves is none of our business. Indeed, it is
impertinent for us to interfere in what does not concern us,
and for us to attempt to do so is to chart the high road to
unpopularity and to render ourselves without influence. We
may do something by force of example, a possibly discourag-
ing thing in the modern world and of limited effectiveness.
One would of course allow that when we have been entrusted
with some proper authority, as of parent, teacher, priest, or
officer of the law, we may properly undertake the reformation
of others within the bounds of reason and judgment. Beyond
these special relations there is nothing to be done about reforming other people as long as they refrain from injuring us
or the community to which we belong and for which we are
responsible—nothing to be done in the way of crusading
against vice and sin in others. The exercise of impertinent
piety, indeed, would seem to be an unrecognized enemy to
moral reform. We must as individuals give over these things
in favor of the study and practice of Christian ethics in its
application to ourselves. The cultivation of the ample terri-
tory of the duties we owe to ourselves and the achievement of
the virtues that are attached to them are enough to keep us

busy and are our only hope. Let us understand that these virtues are strictly our affair and are matters between God and us; and for anybody or for any government to intrude them on us is not only a natural impertinence but, I think, and I think that Milton thought, a natural injustice. Let us note, however, that within this our proper field we have, if we refrain from injury to others, a natural liberty to live and to go about our business. This principle would seem to be a bedrock on which may be built a defense against the tyranny of society over the individual in whatever utopian or totalitarian form it may assume.

The field of the duties one owes to oneself, as also the right to live without injury to others, may be said to be one's natural domain. These are the things that Jefferson declared rather vaguely to be "self-evident," as to be sure they are: that all men are created equal; that they are endowed by their Creator with certain inalienable rights; that among them are life, liberty, and the pursuit of happiness. The partition of duties and the logical inferences to be drawn from it have the effect of shoving the Jeffersonian doctrine one stage further back and of grounding it in the science of ethics and therefore in nature. Nature provides the distinction and bestows on man at his creation a right to liberty of a certain necessary sort if he is to be the creature he was created to be. The distinction between the duties man owes to himself and those that he owes to his fellow men offers a perfect accounting for the doctrine of liberty under the law and illuminates the whole field of the social sciences. It makes exactly clear the nature and limits of man's freedom, his only possible freedom, in civilized society.

For there are no frustrations, no social road blocks, in the way of doing our duty toward our fellow men. The world has never been known to object to the exercise of humanity, good will, compassion, brotherly love, friendship, and generosity. One may go into the street and blow a trumpet announcing that one means to do one's full duty by all human creatures; and, if one is able to substantiate these claims, nobody will object, and one will grow in power and popularity. I take somewhat diffidently by way of illustration the case of the late President Roosevelt. He was perhaps not conspicuous in the field of the duties he owed himself, but in the field of the duties he owed his fellow men he was an irresistible genius. It used to be said that everybody was against him but the electorate.

For the sake of logical completeness may I be permitted to call attention to the principle and domain of the law? Society refuses to be injured and is organized in such a way as to afford to its members protection against injury. To do injury to society or to its members is to infringe the law, and bordering on the field of the duties one owes to one's fellow men lies the whole field of the law. The curriculum of a law school or the docket of a circuit court will show what is involved.

The implications of this distinction in ethics are so far-reaching and so subversive of the ideals and practices of current moral and religious teaching that I hardly dare tell you all that is involved. I shall content myself with saying that an almost complete change in attitude and method is involved and with citing a very few examples for your consideration.

It has already been said, in part by implication, that man is the governor of his own domain and that his rights within that domain are, as Jefferson said, "inalienable," since they rest on the proposition that man, doing no harm to others, has by nature the right to be the creature he was created to be. This he has, if he has any such thing as natural right; and natural right may be, and has been, inferred from the fact of existence and demonstrated in the history of human progress. This doctrine says that self-government, popular government, is not only the best government, but the only government that is in accordance with nature. It displaces tyranny and the

doctrine that man should be governed for his own good.   It
rejects the whole idea of propaganda and so restricts the field
of advertising that the greater part of it is revealed as plain
dishonesty.   Infringement on the liberty to choose becomes
immoral, because there are no morals except those that rest
on voluntary choice.   This doctrine of liberty tells us, for
example, why Prohibition did more harm in this country than
liquor had ever done and actually rendered almost universal
the evil it sought to suppress.   The doctrine strikes a deadly
blow at much evangelism, for it seems to say quite simply,
"The salvation of my soul is my own affair."   Certain attitudes
and practices in college and university teaching are seen, not
only as impertinent, but as offensive and stultifying.   We must
be prepared to agree that in higher education we responsible
officials would do a better and a sounder job if we put the
matter of getting an education squarely up to our students,
and let it go at that.   If we had the resolution, the backbone,
to refuse recognition to anything but achievement, our success would certainly be greater.

    A student in college owes it to himself, and not to his
teachers, his parents, or his country, to be temperate, sober,
chaste, modest, decent, contented, frugal, liberal, industrious,
and magnanimous.   When he moulds his conduct in accordance with this pattern, he is serving himself and nobody else.
Let us see if we can make this matter clear.

    In colleges and universities we have a situation in which, as
Woodrow Wilson put it in his Dartmouth College speech,
"The sideshow has swallowed the circus."   Extracurricular
activities of all kinds, justified by false prophets even among
faculty members, have been declared more important than
curricular activities and have so crowded in on us that to be
studious in college is no longer a normal, much less an inevitable, way of spending a student's time.   Study, like every other
good work in this world, has to be contrived.   This outside
interference with the function of the college or university is a

nuisance and worse, but, although difficult, it is nevertheless still possible for a student to study in college. To study in college or university is to operate functionally in that environment. If one does study, one derives the special benefits that colleges and universities are able to bestow. It is possible to get, as we say, a great deal out of a college education.

I have sometimes asked myself why religious students, a group in whom I have taken great interest, are often inferior. When they are so, the answer is perfectly plain. It is because they are poor students. Study is the public and private duty of college and university students. The religious group, if they are genuinely religious, ought to lead the institution in studiousness. If they did, most of their other difficulties would be overcome. They would belong to the upper twenty or twenty-five per cent of their classes and would therefore, according to averages, amount to something later in life. They would thus, as alumni, powerfully affect the future of the college or university to which they belong. Empty conferences, constant preoccupation with members of the other sex, inept and uninteresting social life, inadequate and ignorant leadership would soon give way among students of high intellectual attainments and practices, for what our colleges and universities and the communities they are supposed to serve need as much as anything else is a larger body of college men and women who move on a really high intellectual level. Studiousness on the part of religious students would soon gain the respect of the institution as a whole. All students would respect the religious group and seek to be associated with them. It would bring religion into higher repute in student bodies and the academic world as a whole. Evangelical activities and membership campaigns would be greatly simplified.

I have chosen to draw my illustration from my friends, from a group of students on whom I place great hope. How easy it would be for me to apply this doctrine of work to other groups for whom I have much less respect!

Postscript

IN REVIEWING the lectures contained in this volume the author recognizes that some at least of the subjects treated are very old interests with him; but, since they were all current interests within the year, he would like to add a paragraph (slightly adapted to the present purpose) from one of his more important addresses, "Shakespeare and the Here and Now," delivered before the Modern Language Association at its Detroit meeting in December, 1951. In it there may perhaps be found a basis of unification of a seemingly unrelated group of essays:

"If one understands that thinking or the formation of concepts is a cerebral act within a space-time continuum, it would be no wild conjecture to suggest that the act would be achieved in terms of better or worse or, one might say, in terms of ideals pursuant of one principle through a mental complex. One might even suggest that the efficiency of the action and the merit of its outcome would depend on the value of its components, that is, on the clarity and vigor with which a given mind might perceive the elements and effect the union. It would follow that the incredibly vigorous and inclusive mind of Shakespeare would create concepts of superior form and superior significance. Successive events of the so-called space-time continuum of physical reality seem to enter as a stream of mental impressions into the brain and to be brought into comparison there with concepts of the absolute. In the general mental process, of which this development is one phase, there may be observed analogies to the physical transformation of kinetic energy into potential energy and vice versa. The point of application of this analogy is found in the fact that the genius of Shakespeare (or Milton or Burns) was able to distinguish clearly the essential difference between varying circumstance and unchanging truth or ideal. In other words, his superior mind could discern the workings of universal law in all aspects of living, no matter how great the diversity of circumstance, in a given current of events. The resulting excellence would not be subject to debilitation, as is material substance, but would be perpetually self-sustaining and inexhaustibly abundant. With regard to the time element, we may consider also the reasoning that the past still exists, not only as an integral part of the present in the sense that truth is ageless and universal, but also in the sense that accumulated knowledge is, either potentially or actively, an ever-present influence in the course of events. When we say that Shakespeare merged himself with Julius Caesar and his Roman contemporaries and entered into their hearts and lives, we are saying the wrong thing. What Shakespeare did can be better described by saying that he brought Caesar and Brutus to London, so that they lived again in London at the Globe."

If we give them the opportunity, Lucian, Shakespeare, Milton, and Burns can obliterate time and resuscitate truth. Whether lectures such as these can facilitate the process is a matter of doubt and contingency.

H. C.